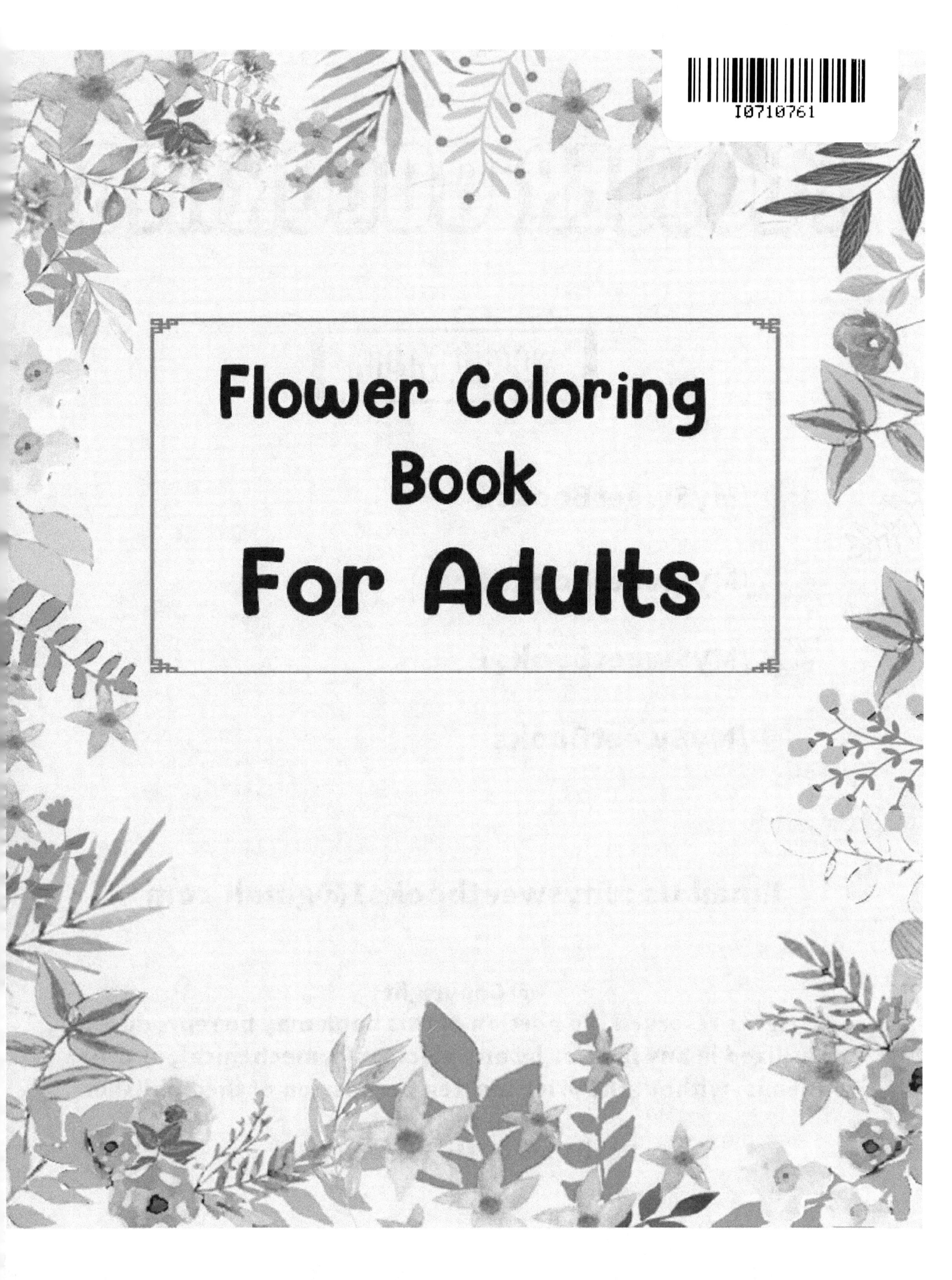

Flower Coloring Book
For Adults

FLOWER COLORING

SOCIAL MEDIA

- f /MySweetBooks1
- /MySweetBooks1
- /MySweetBooks1
- /MySweetBooks

Email Us : mysweetbooks1@gmail.com

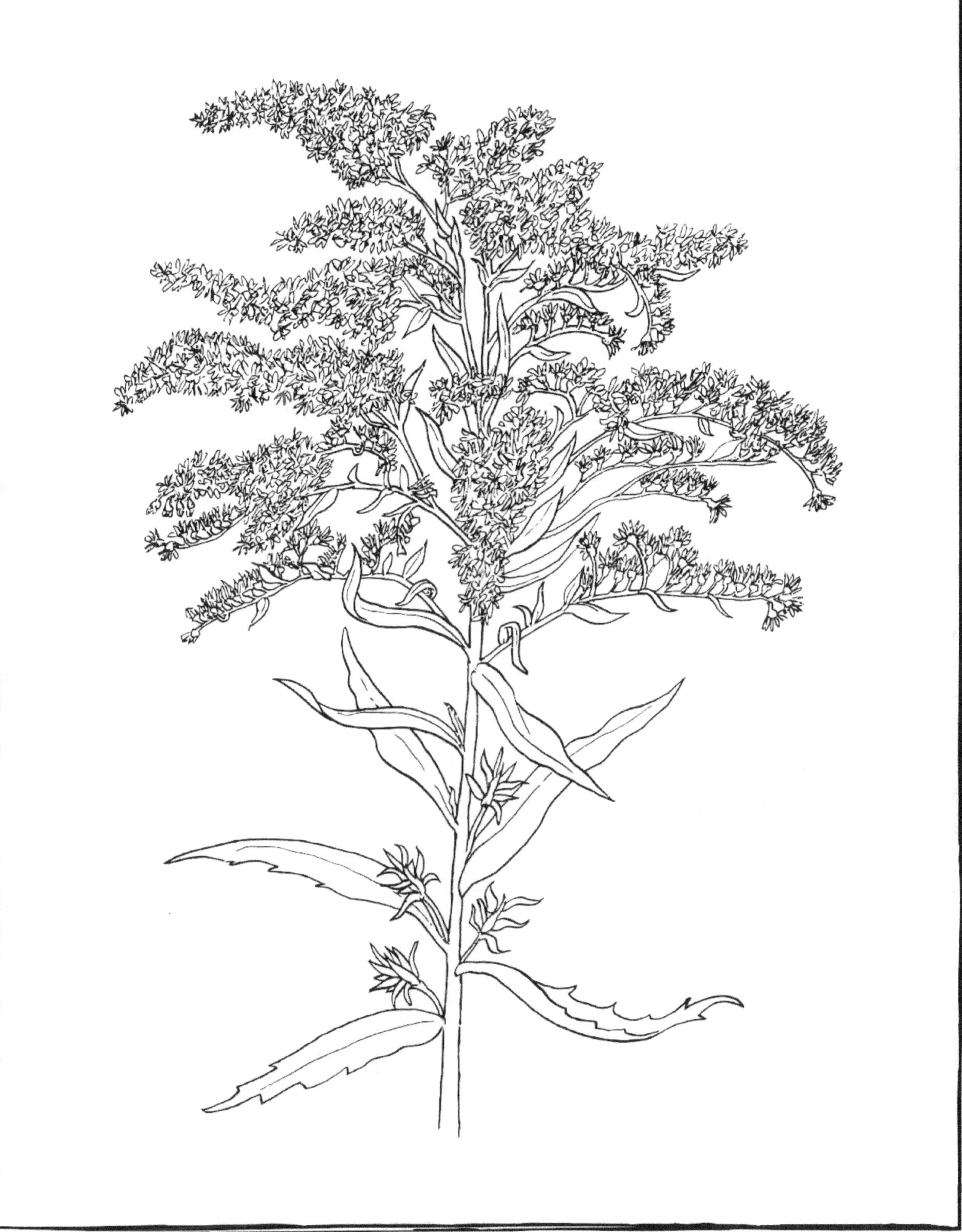

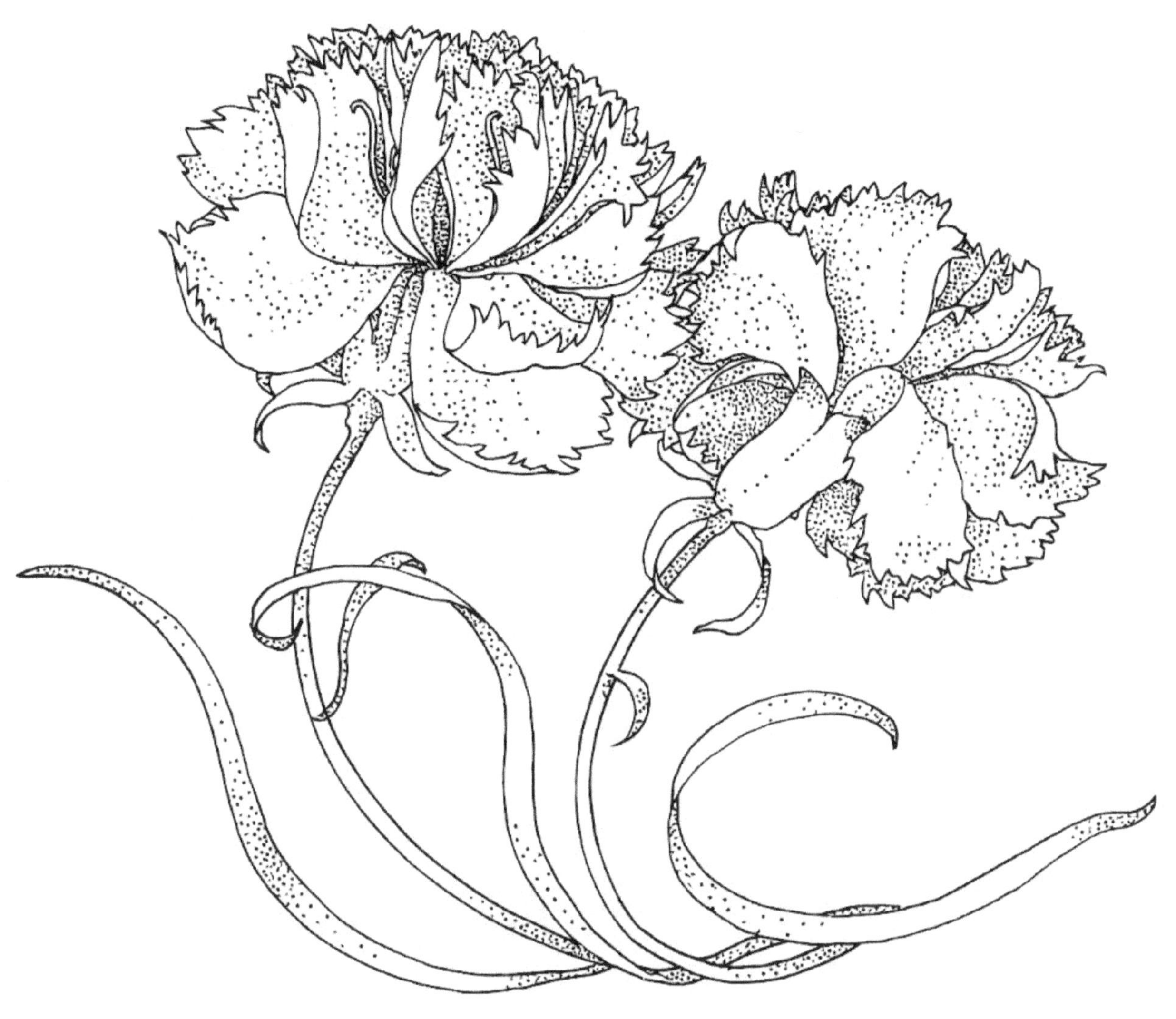

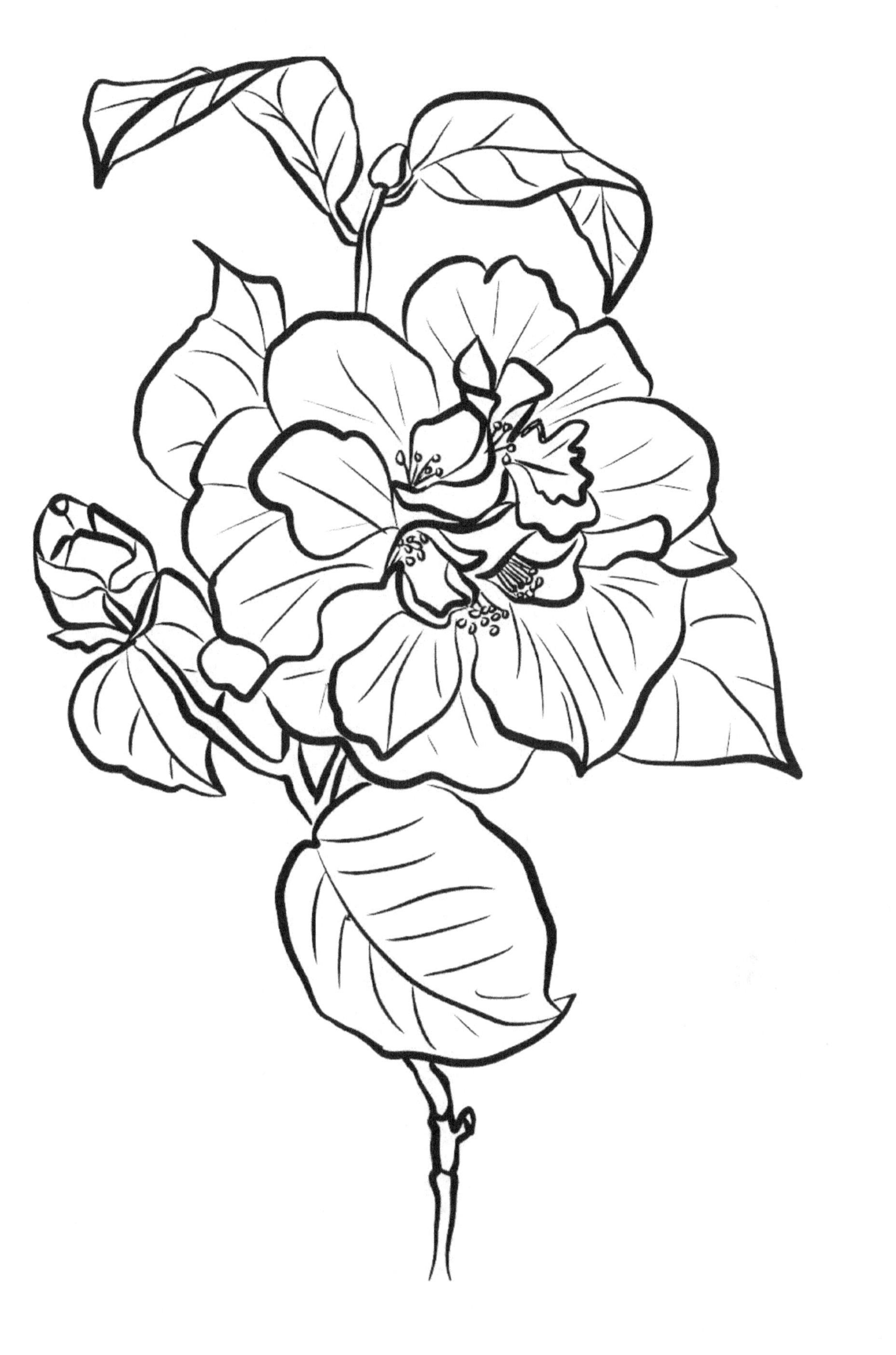

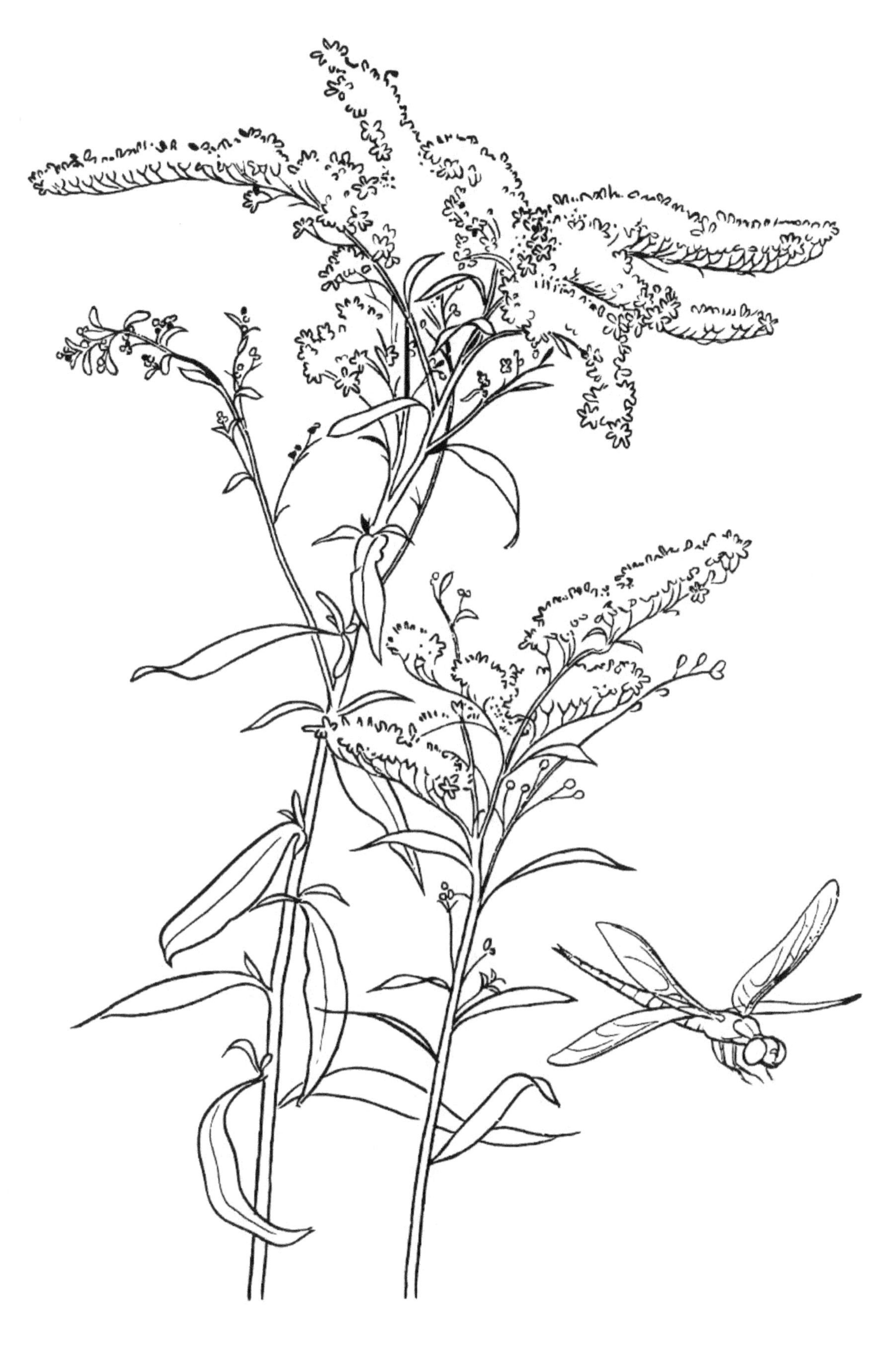

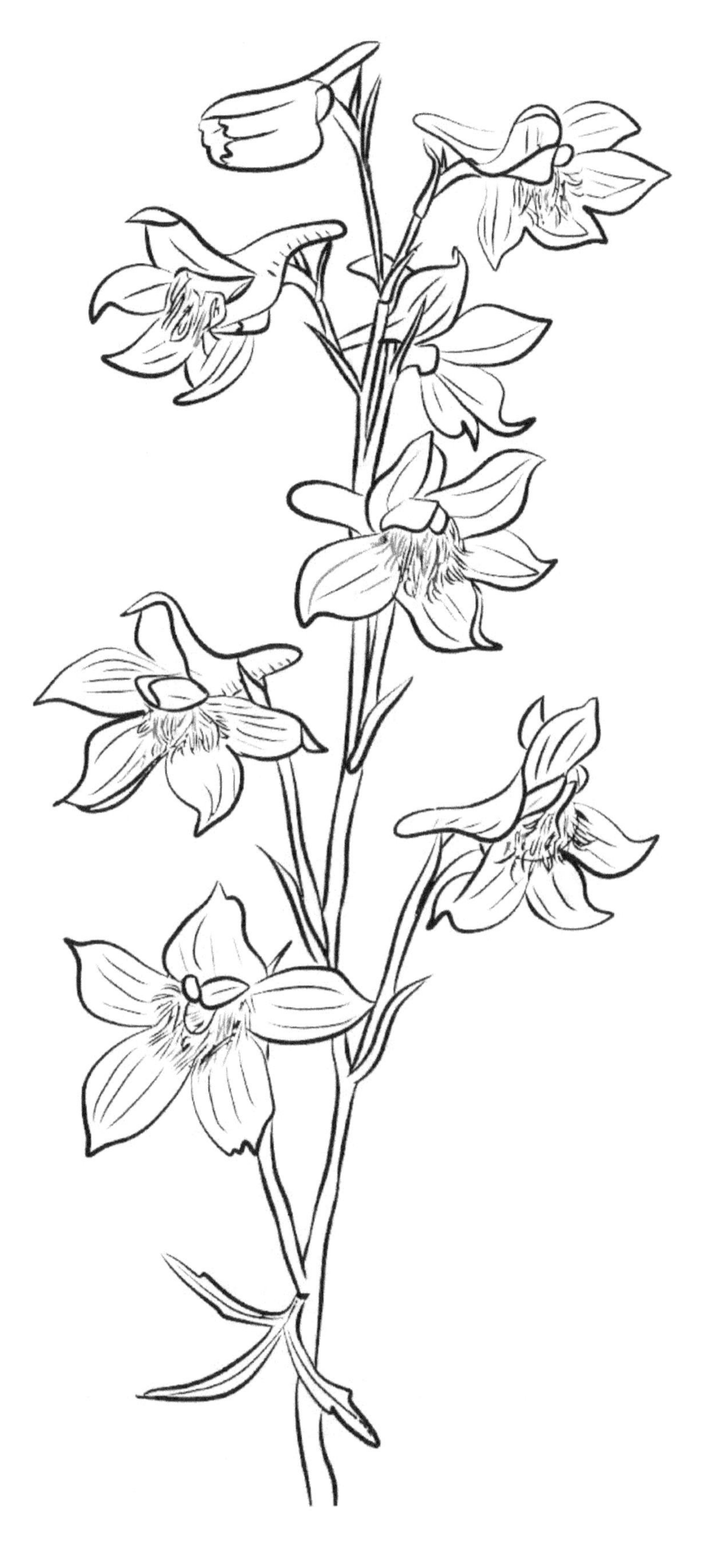

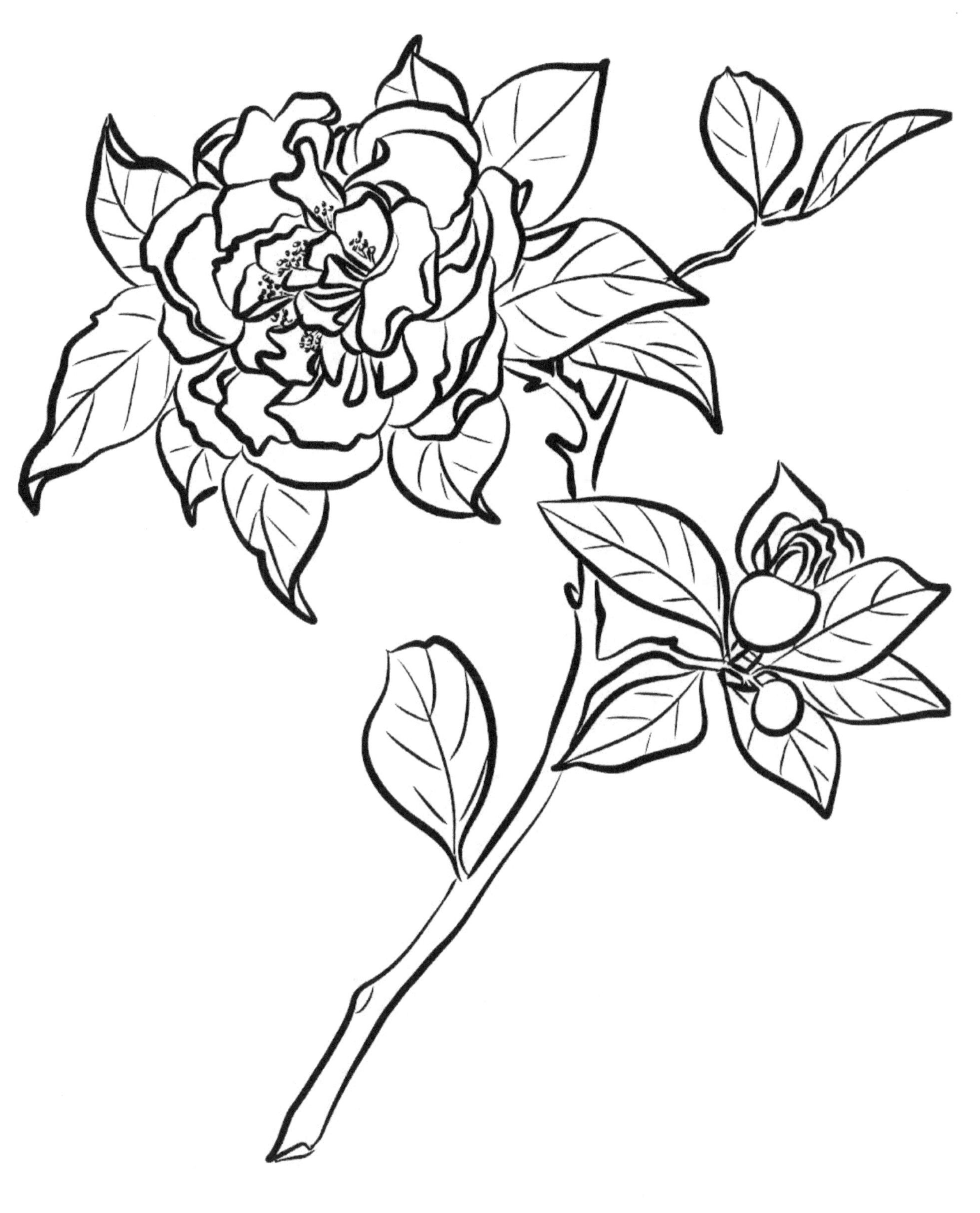

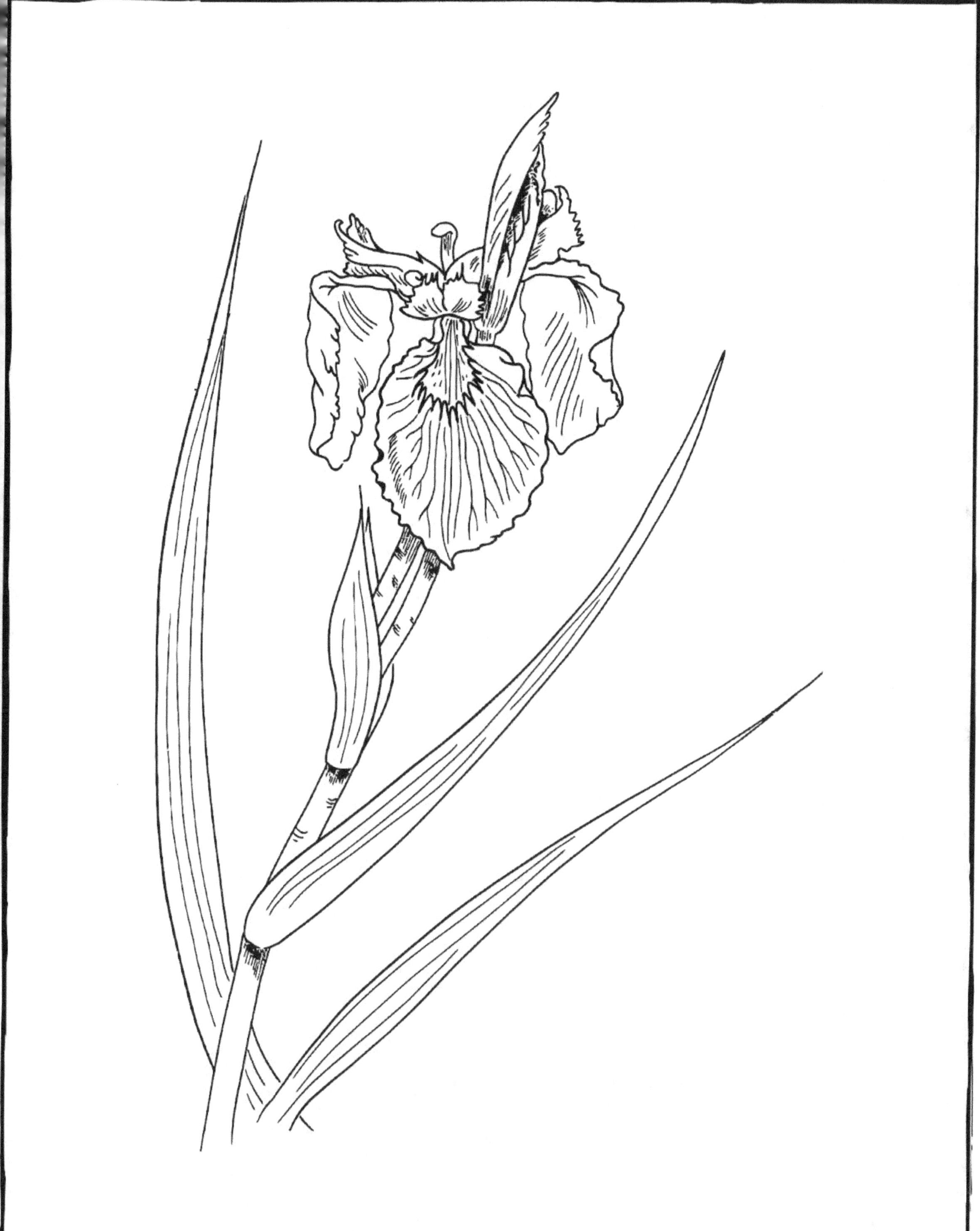

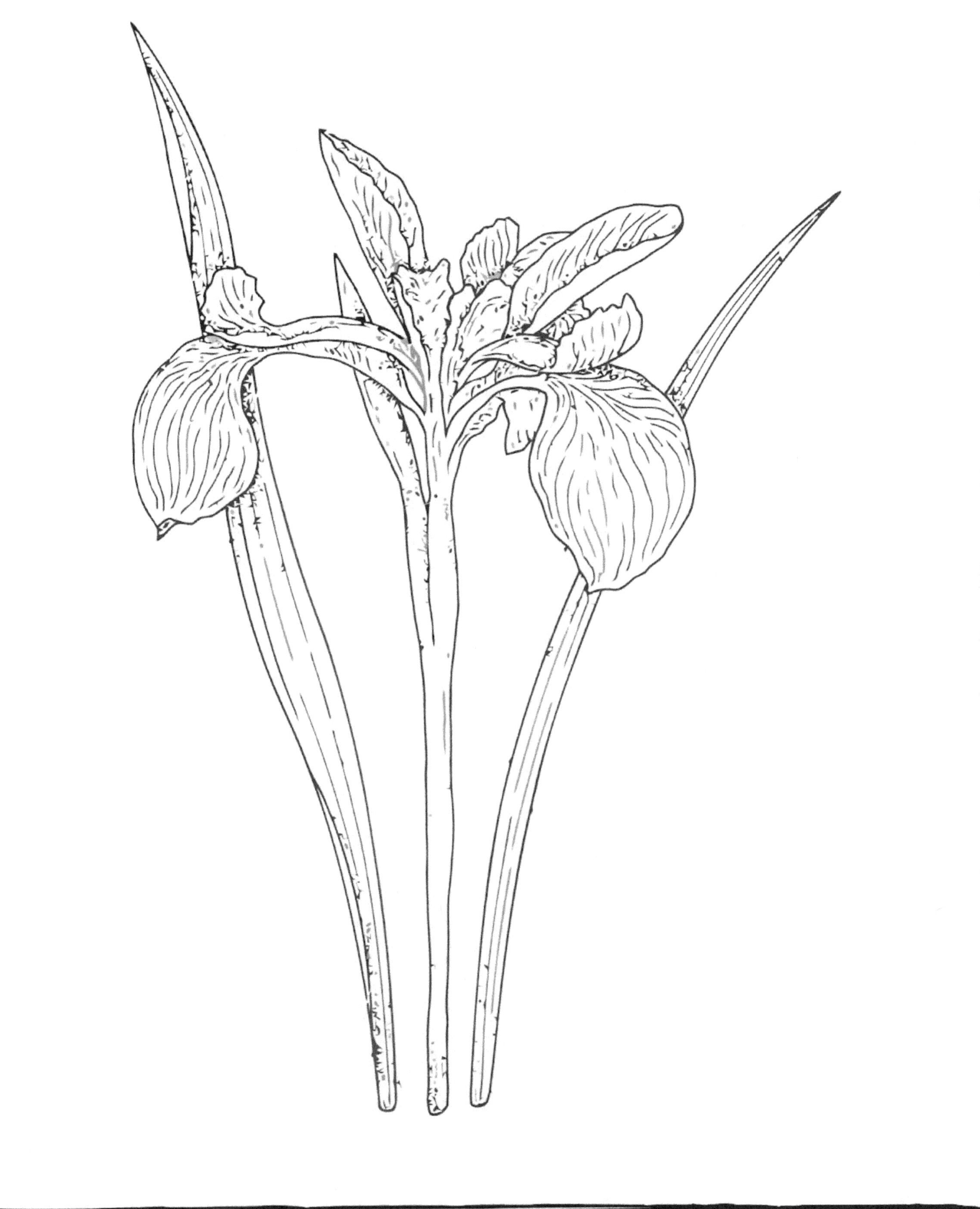

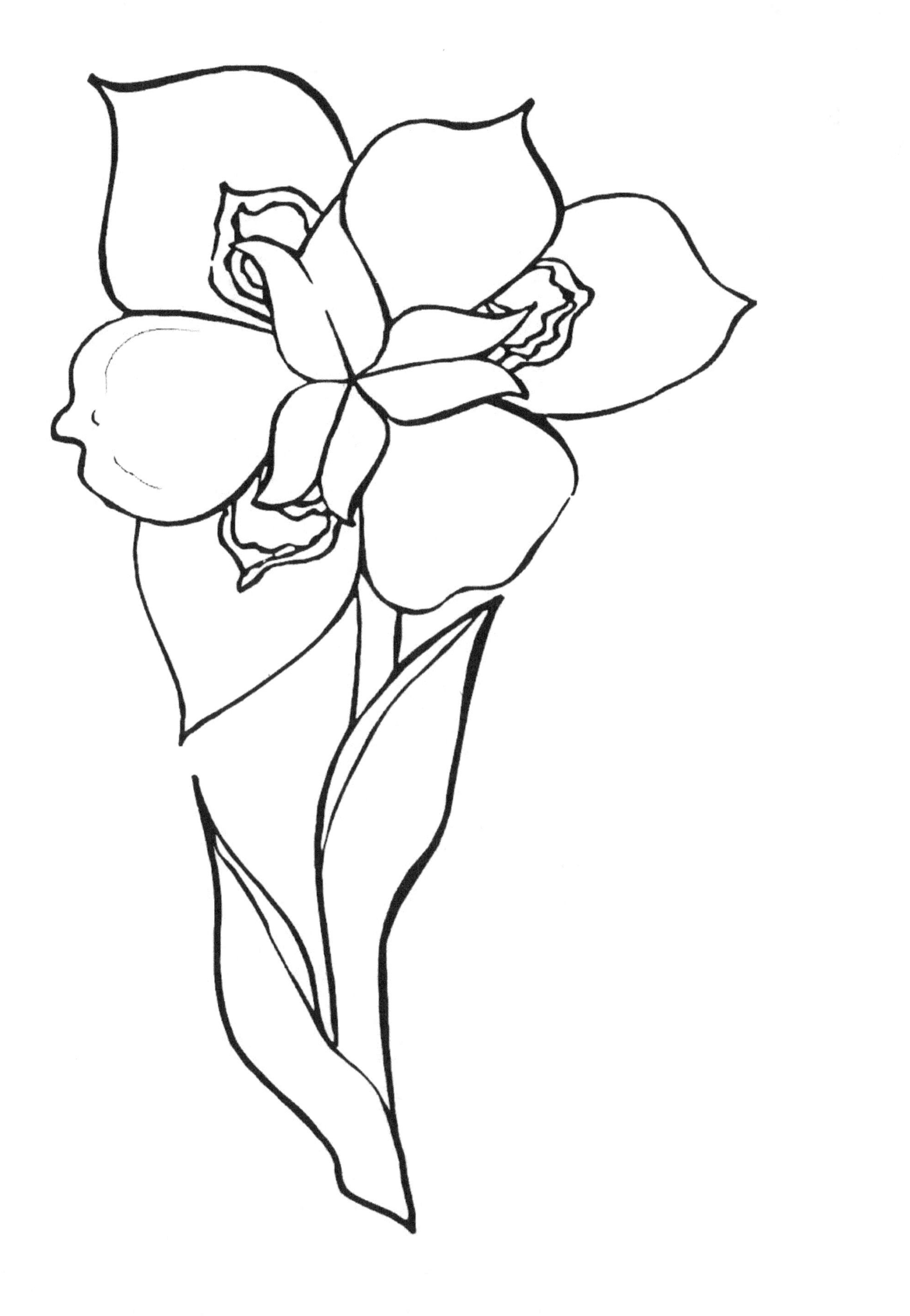

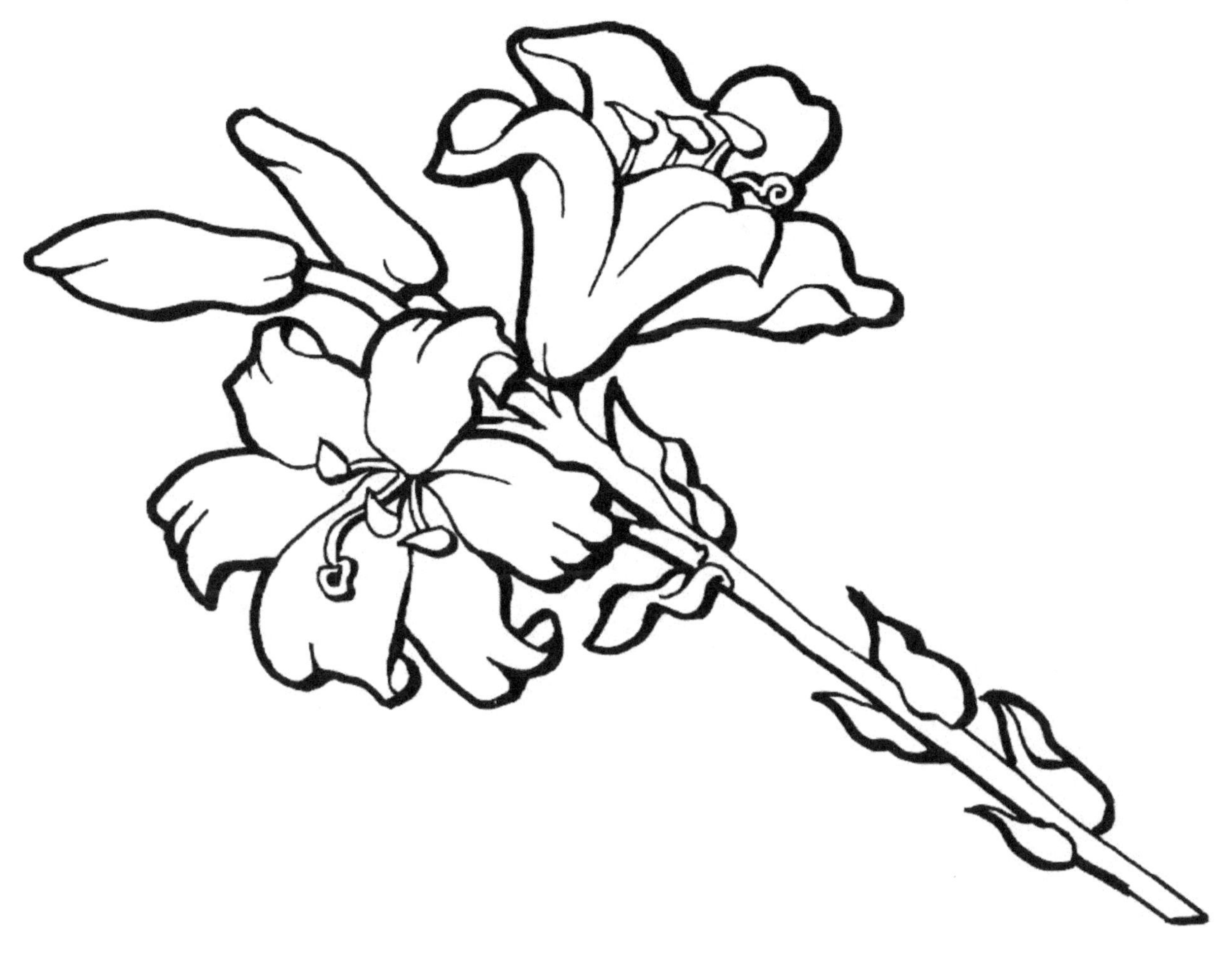

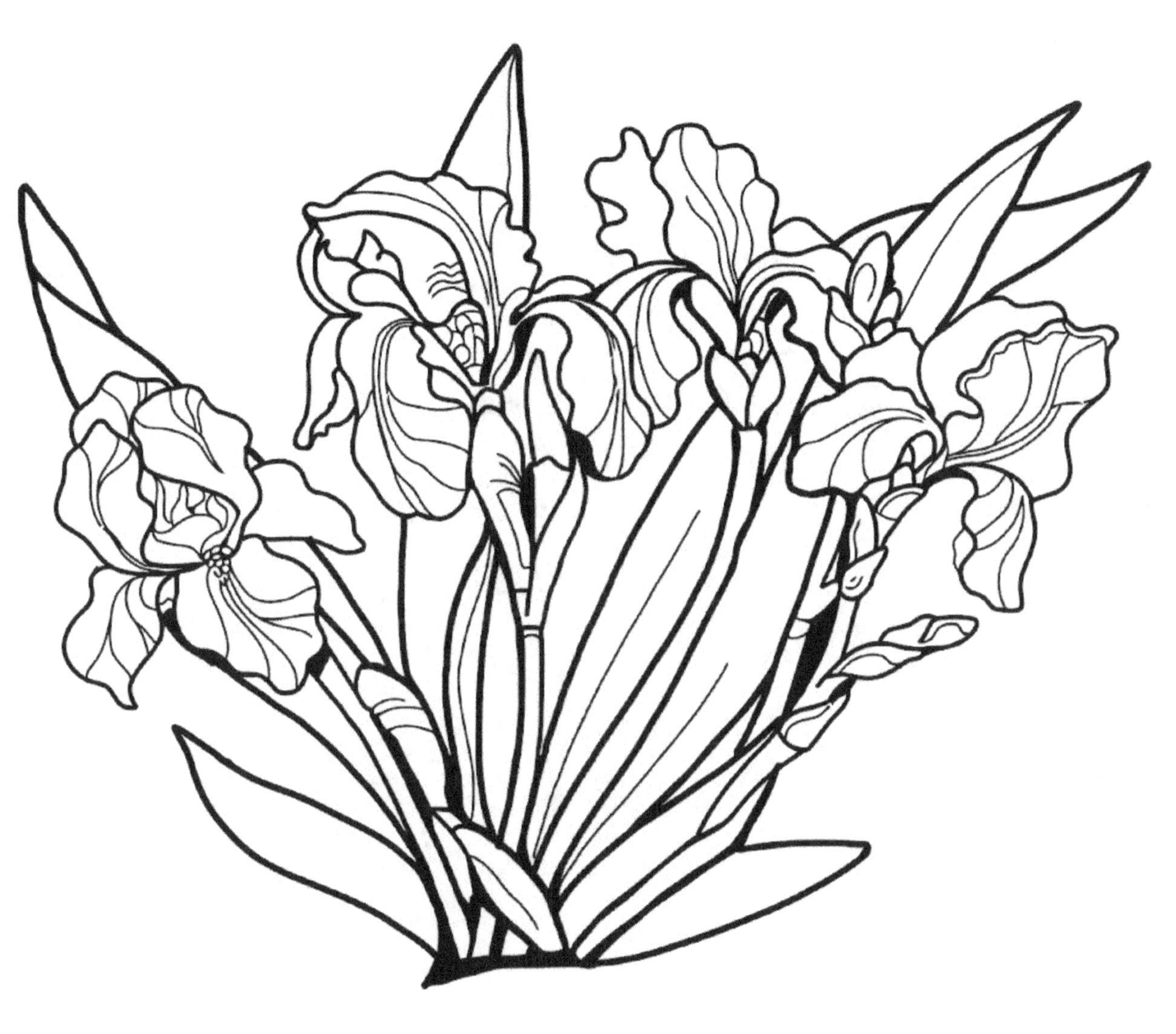

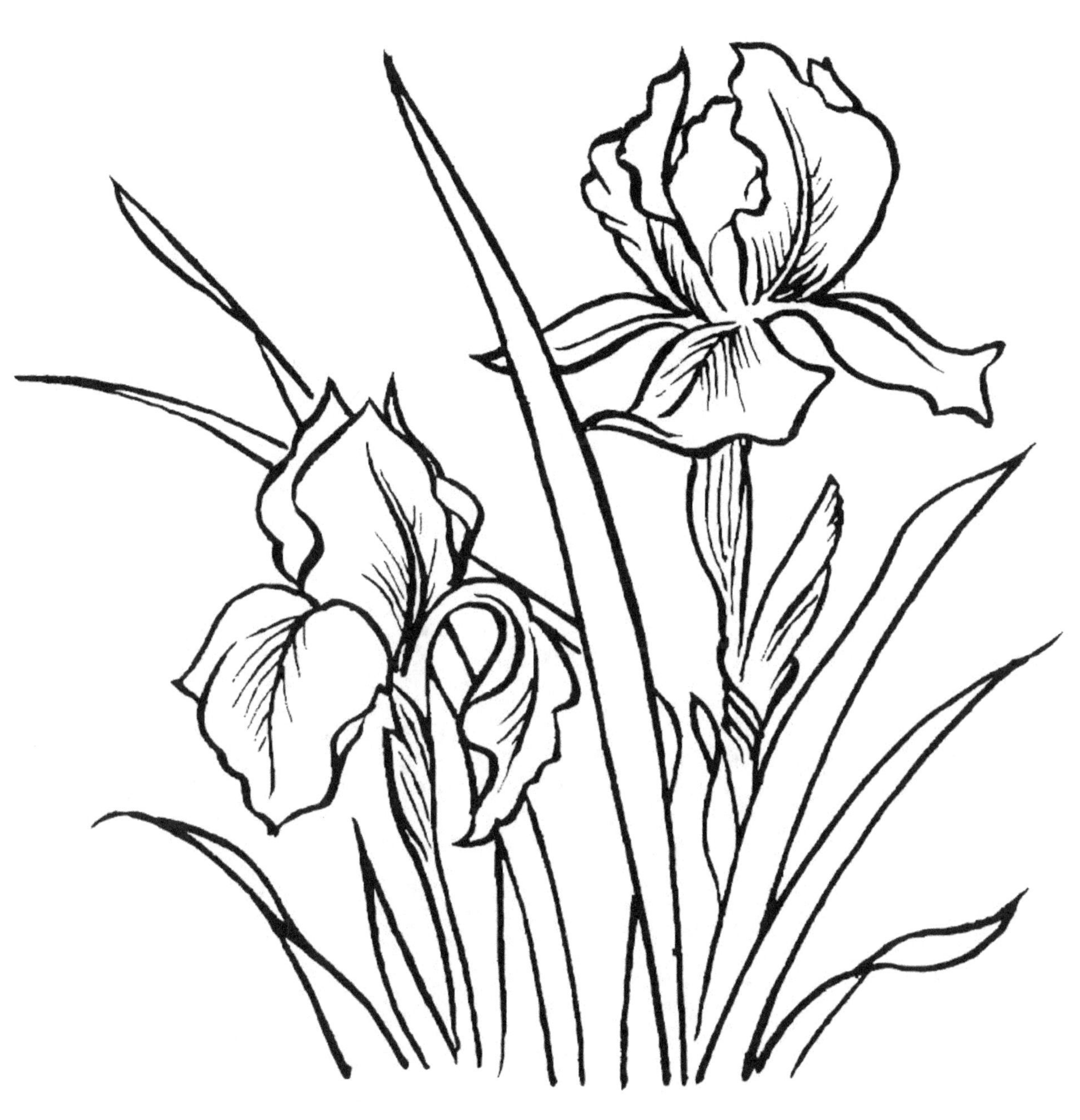

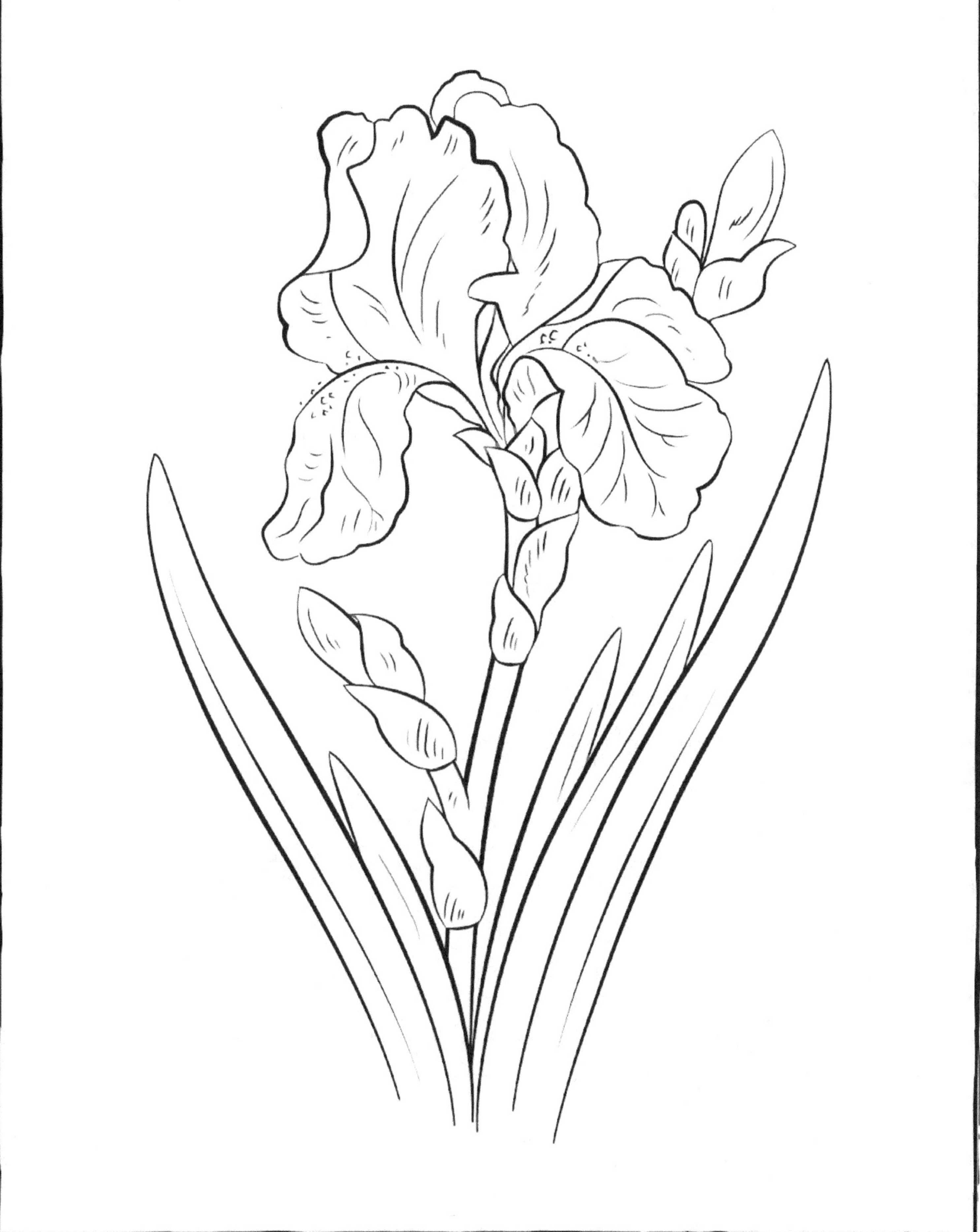

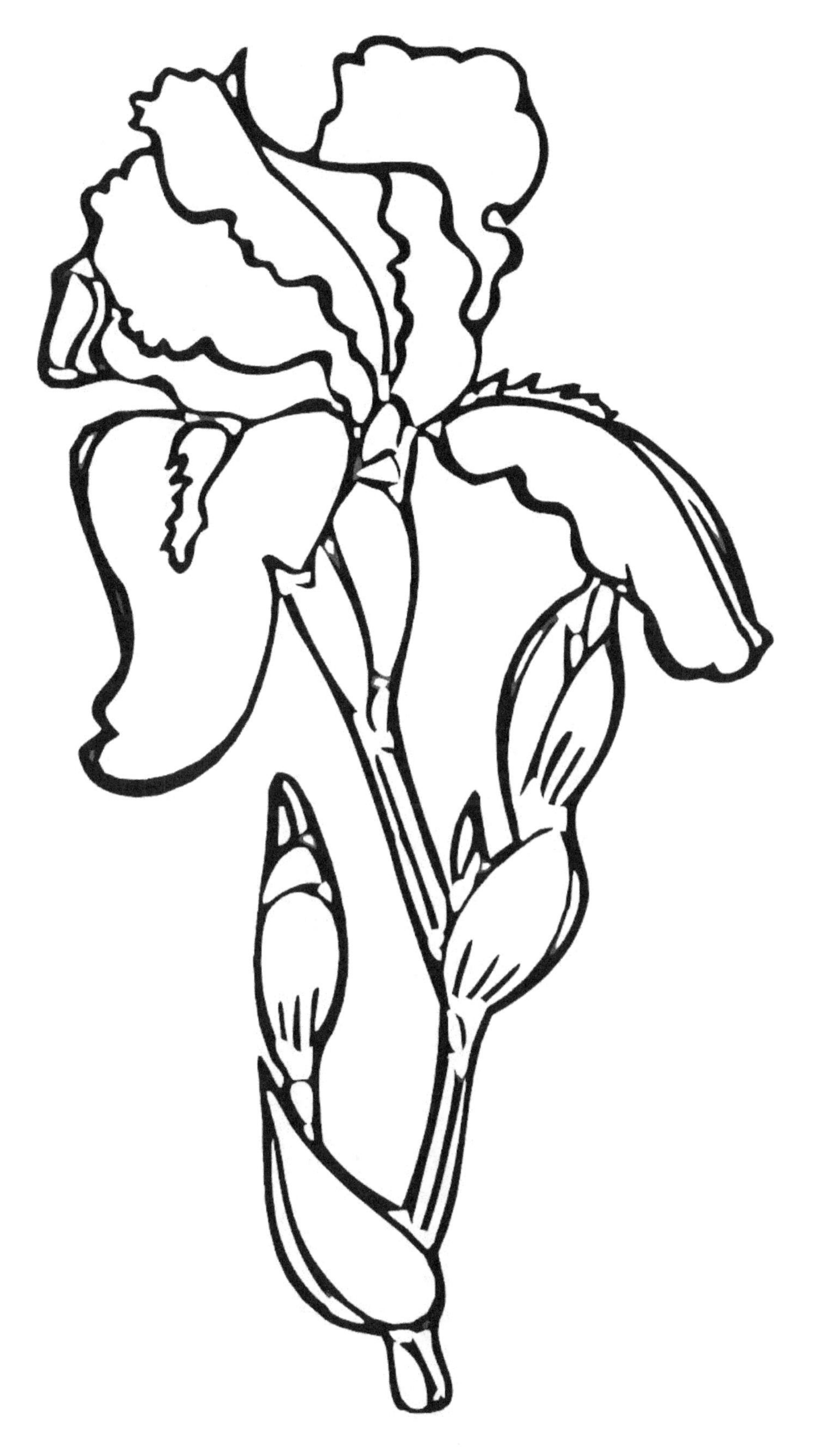

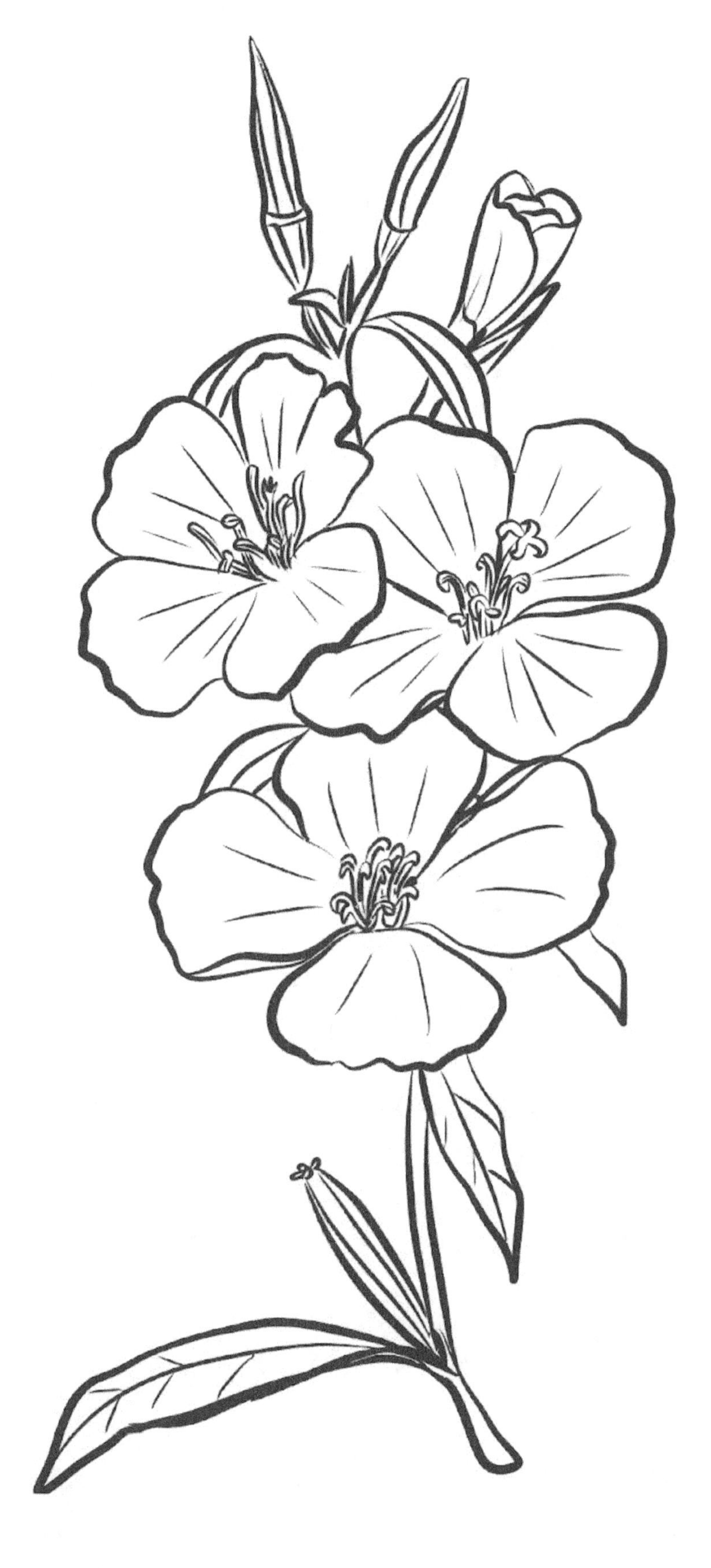

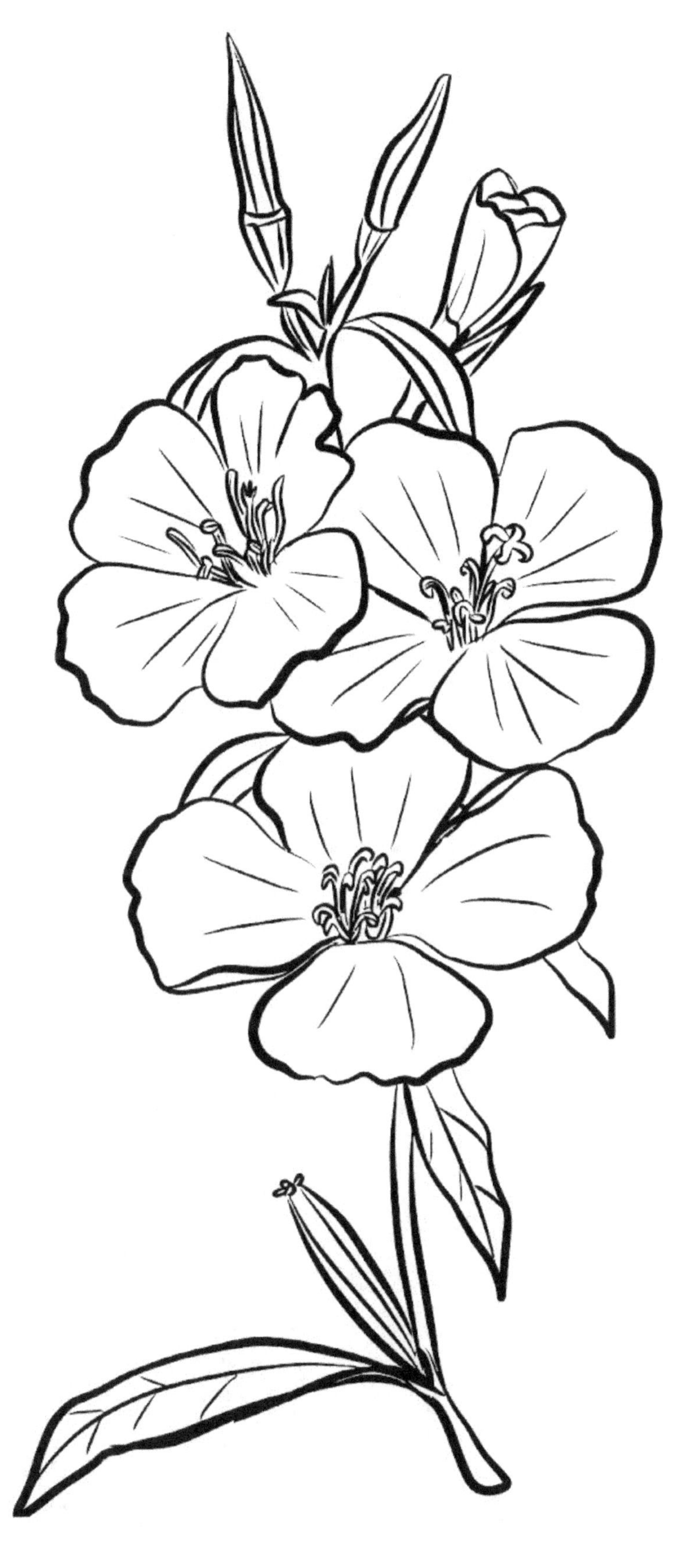

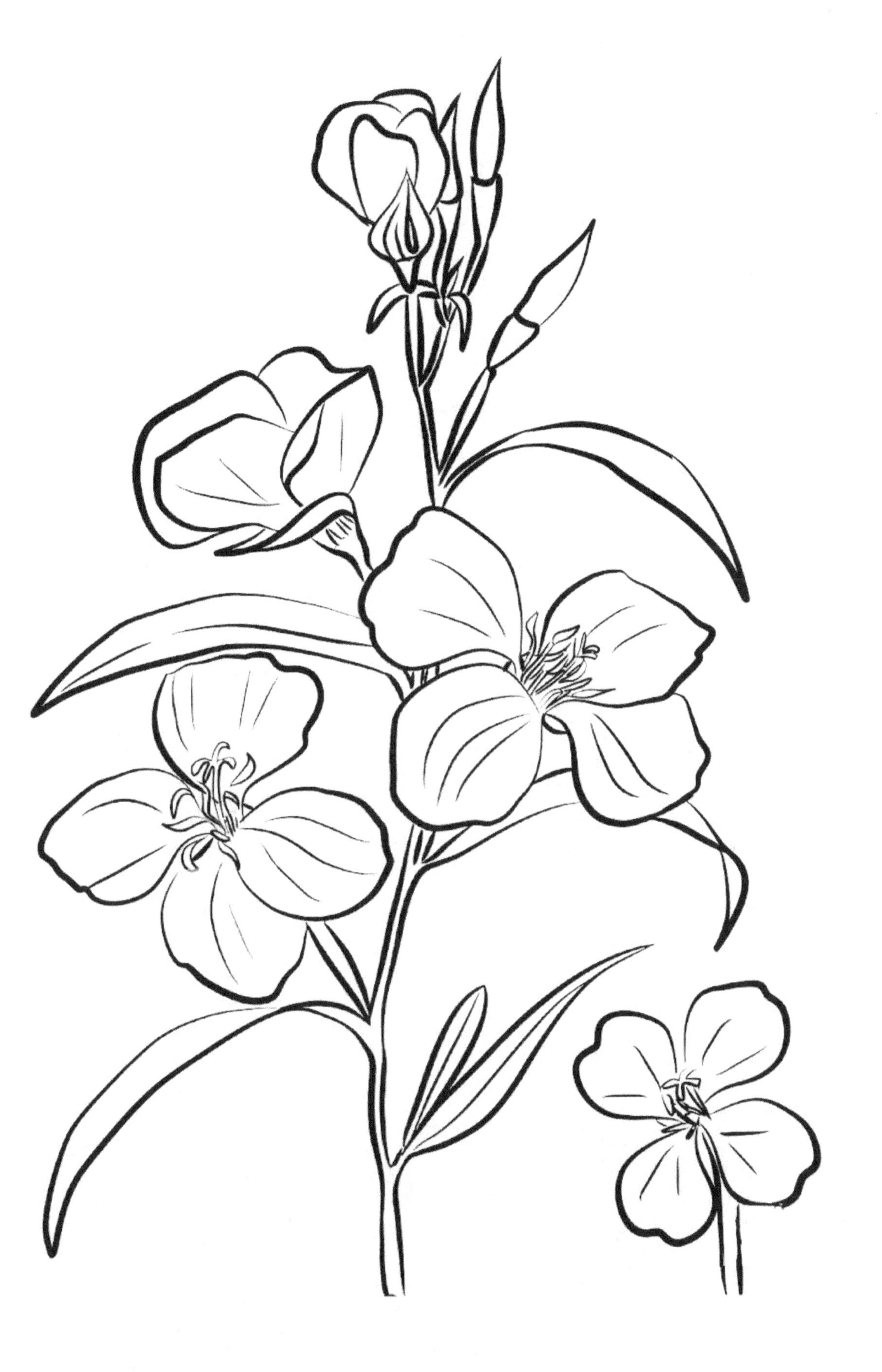

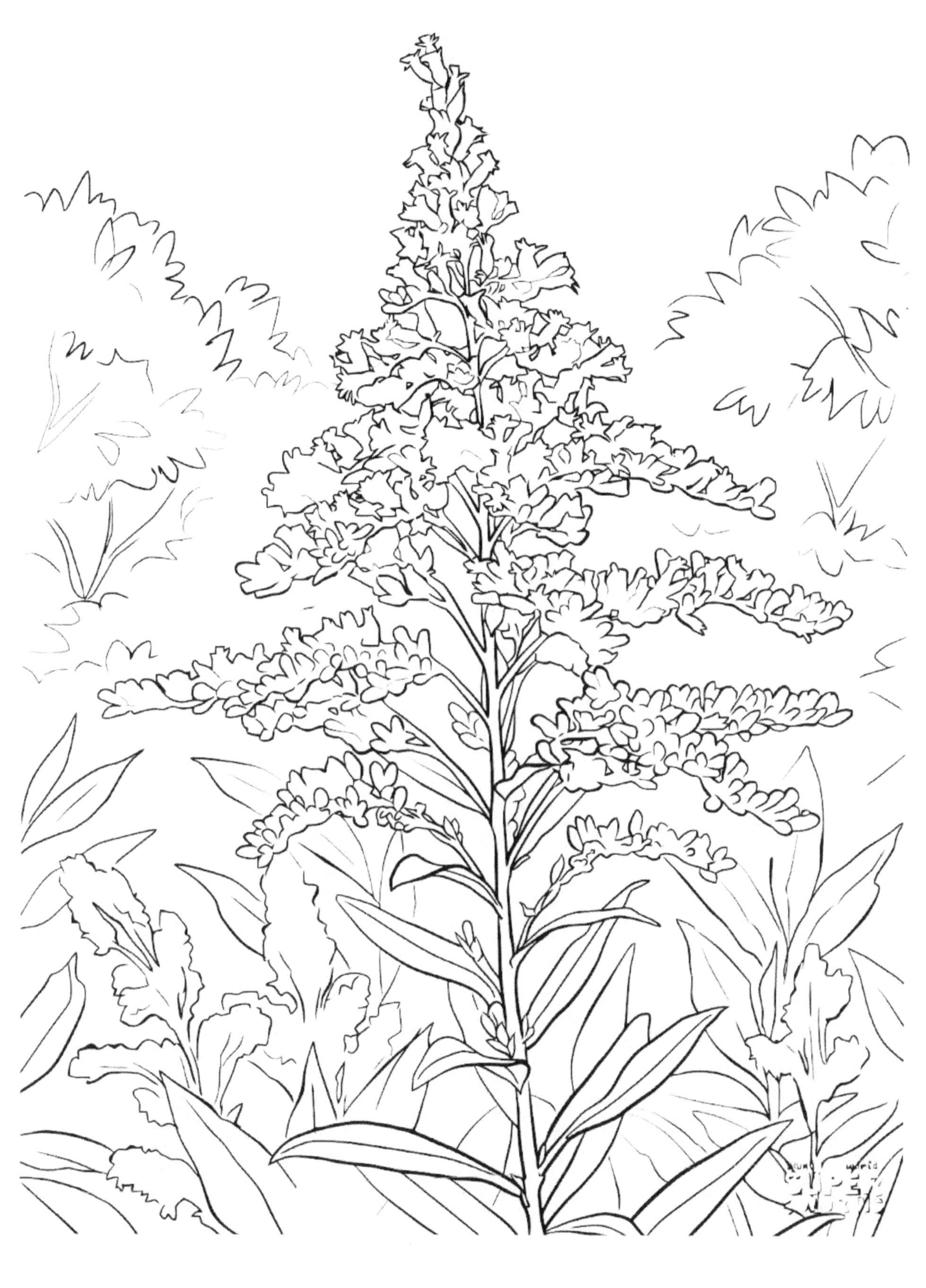

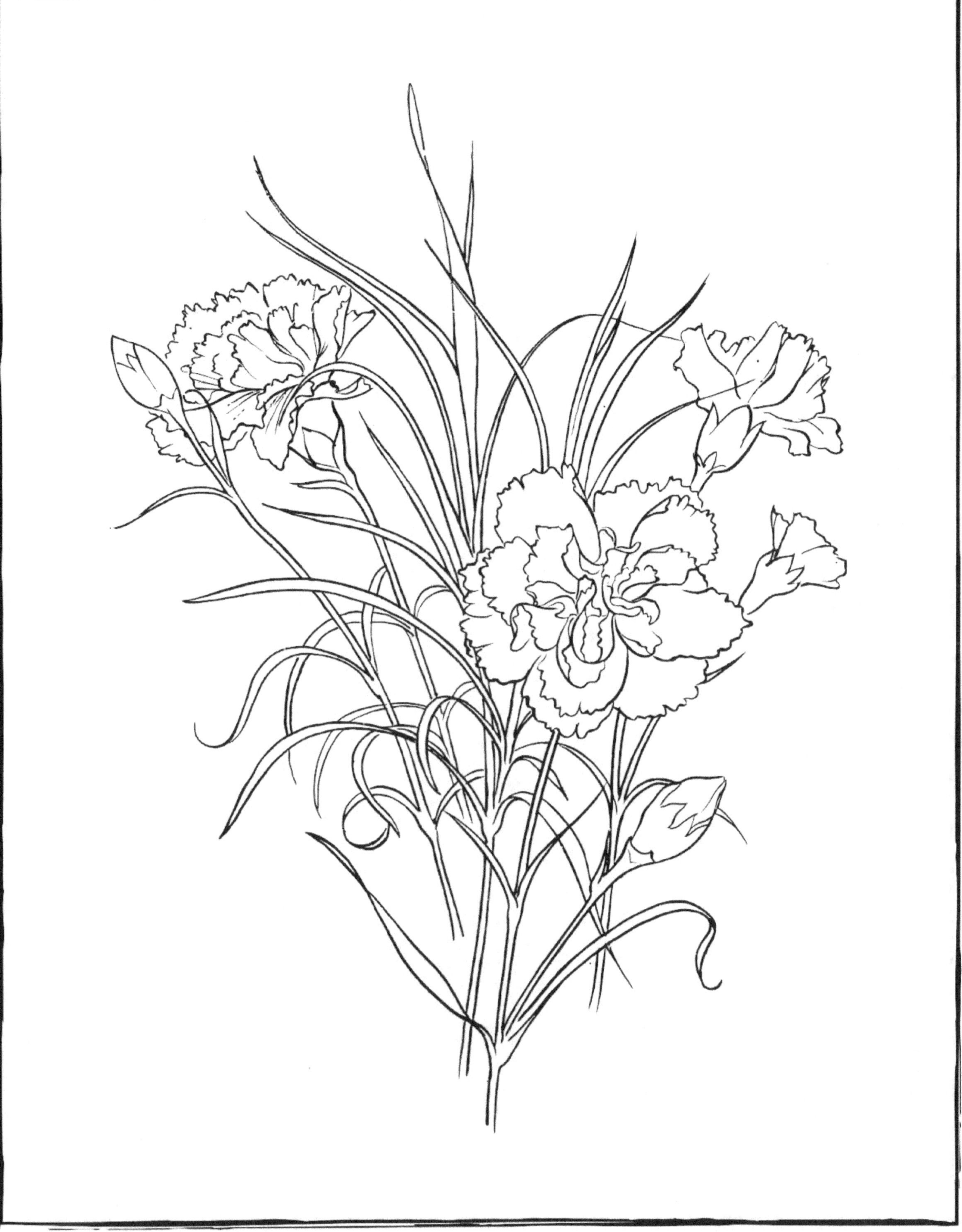

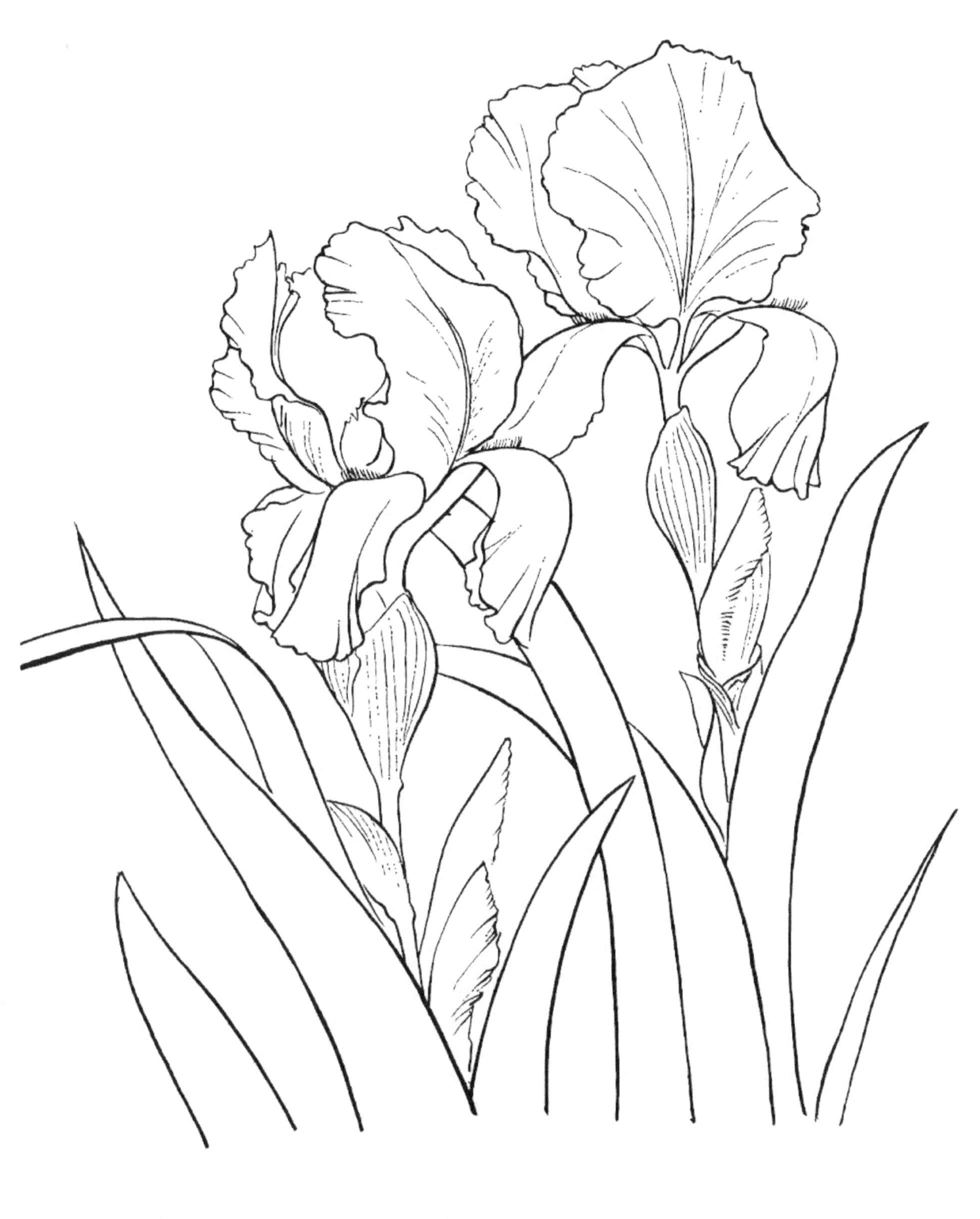

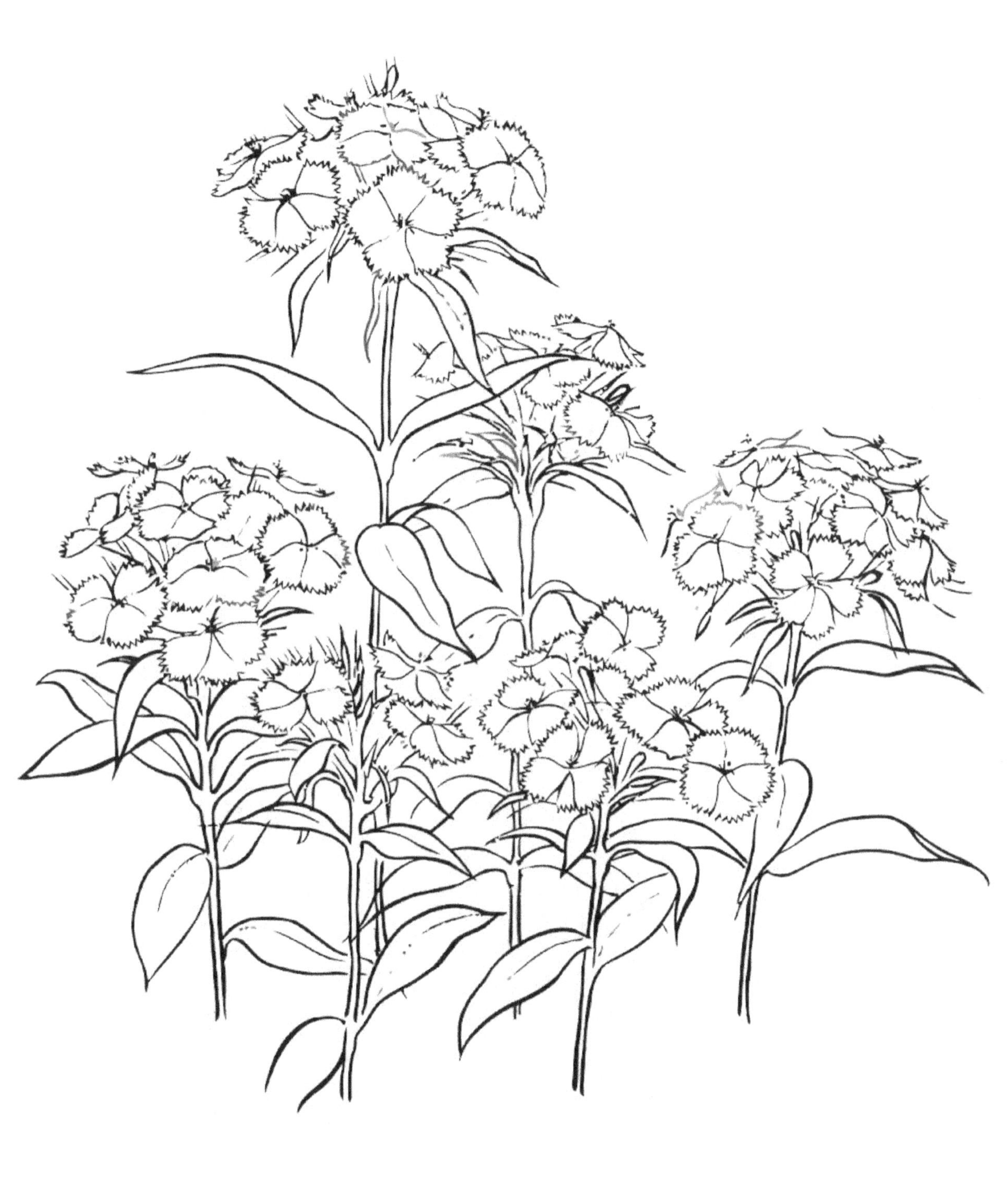

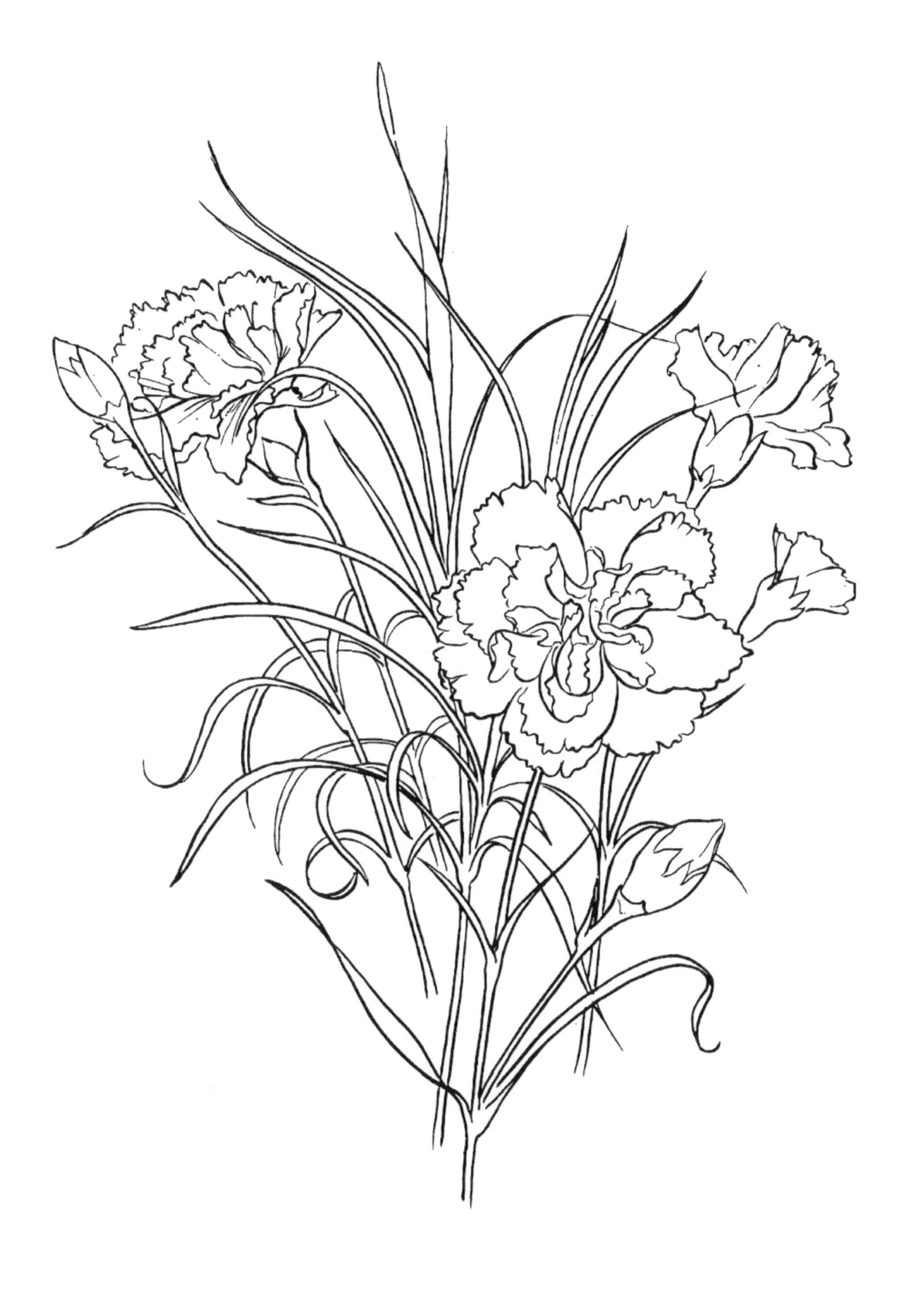

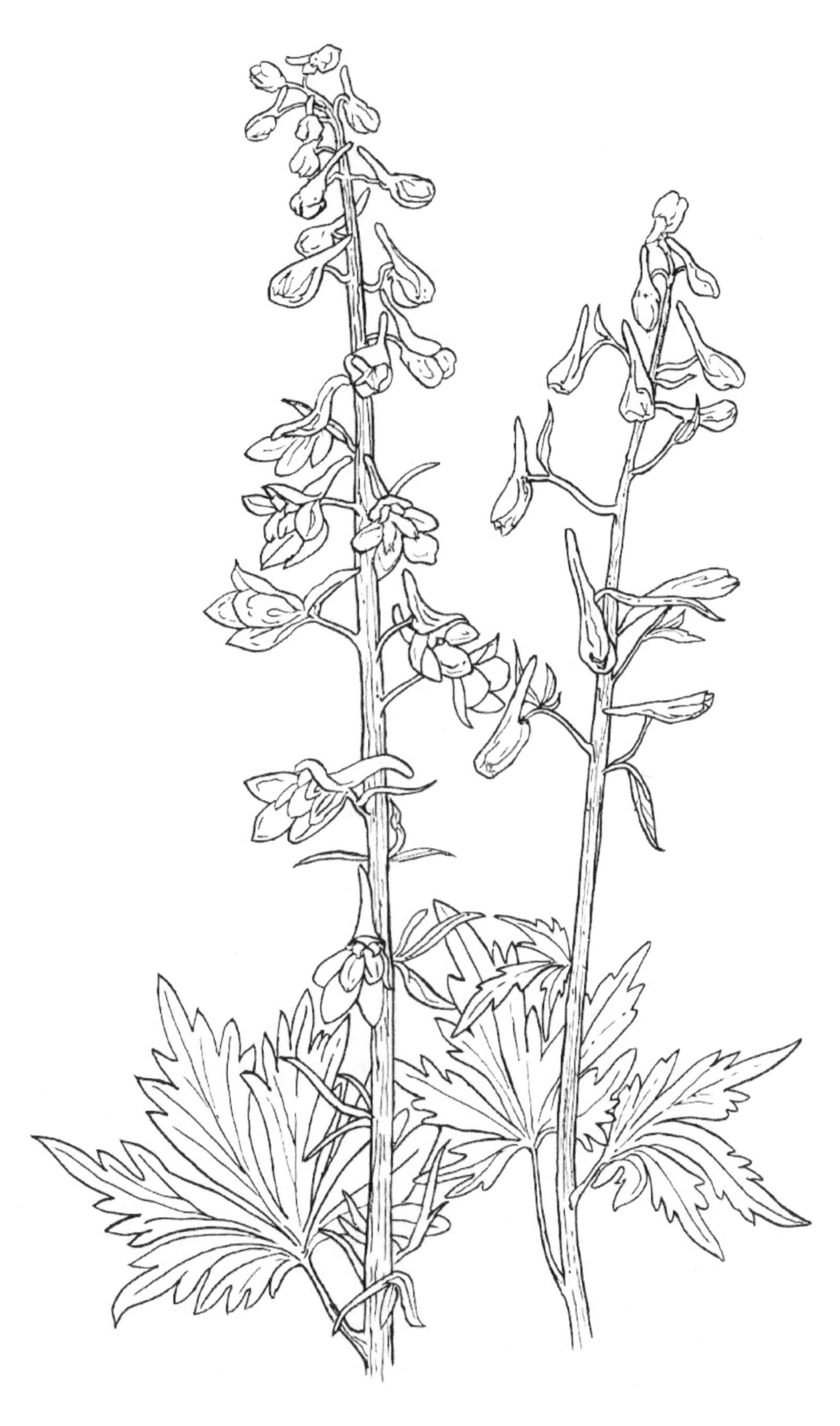

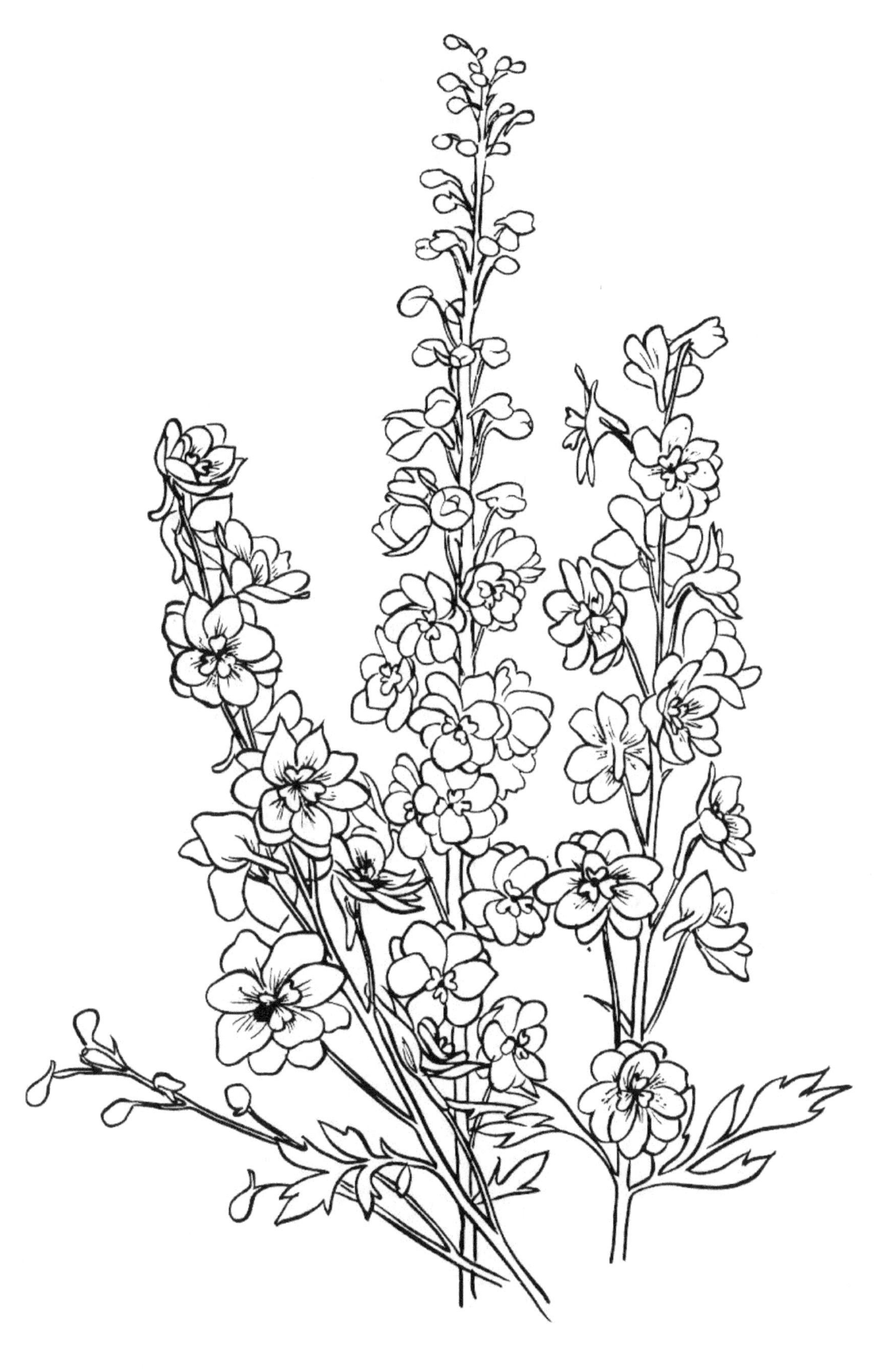

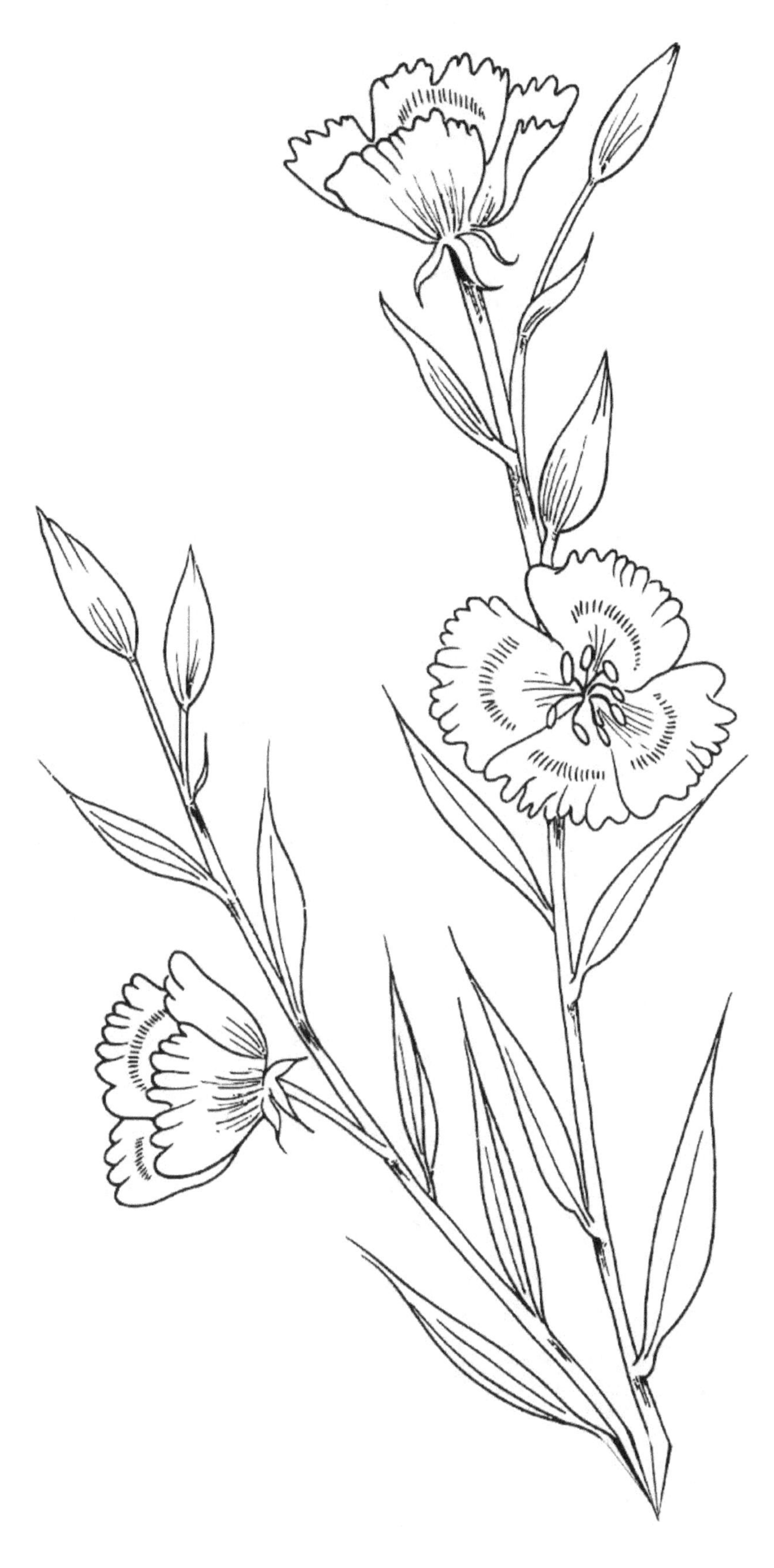

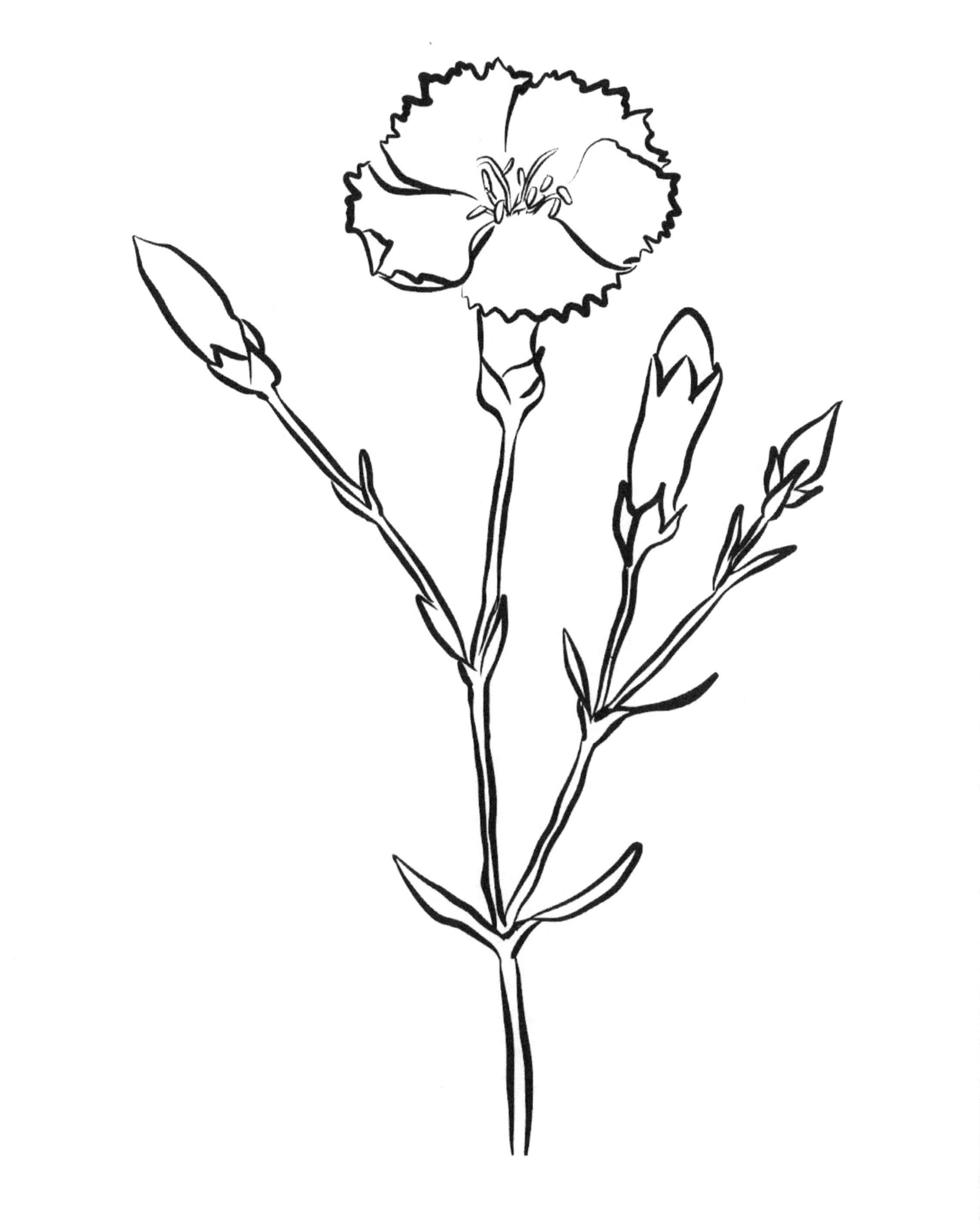

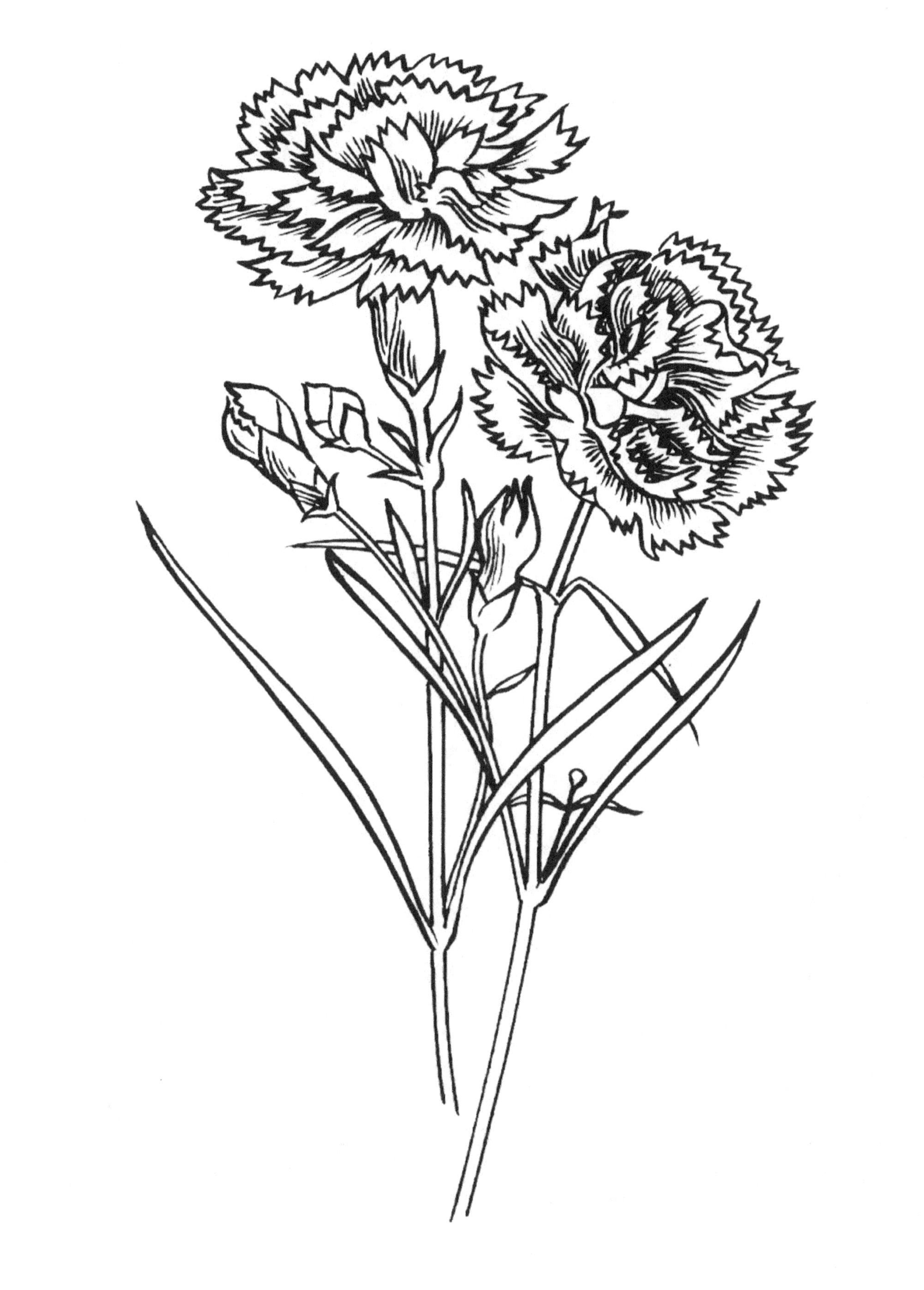

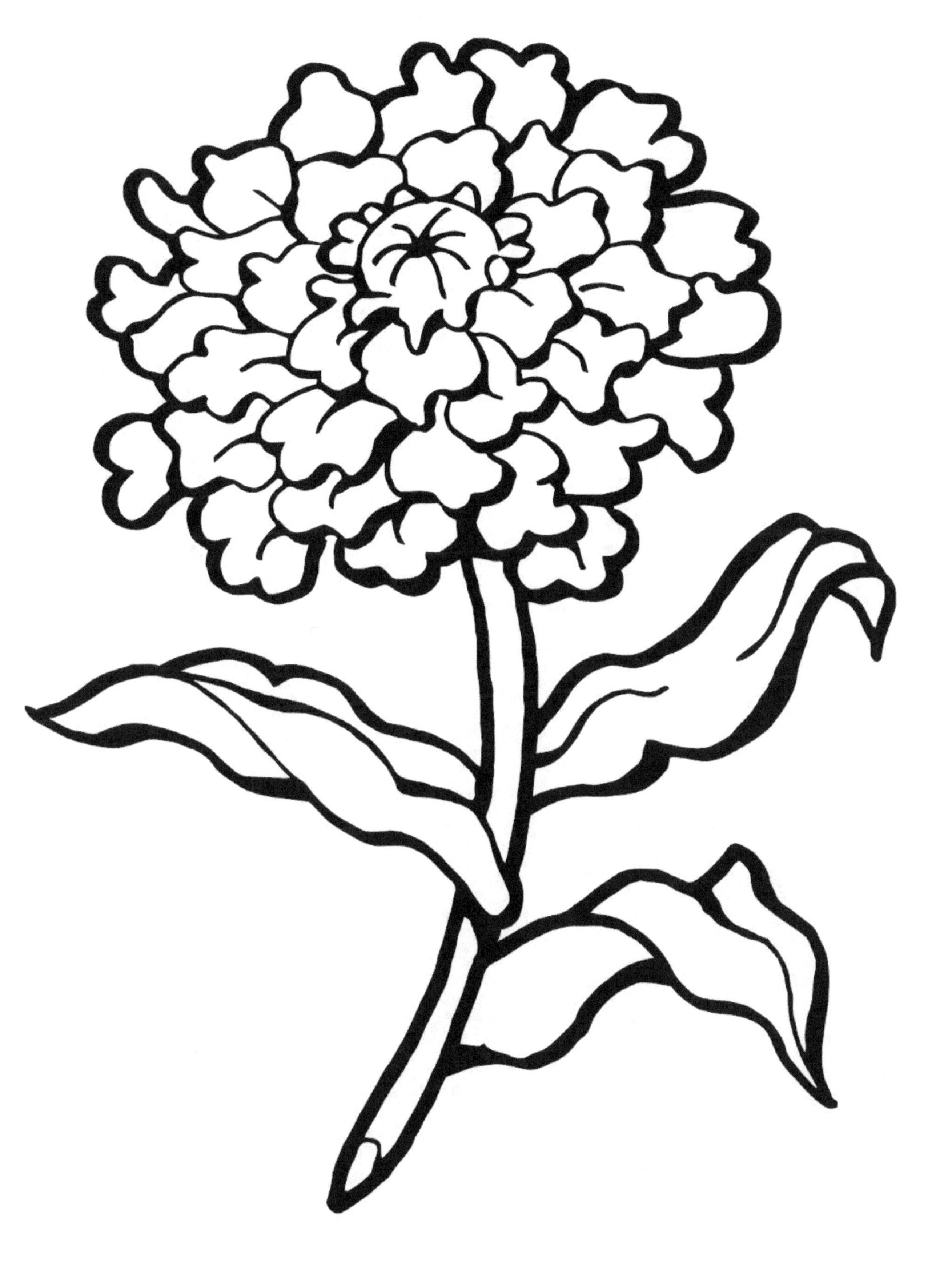

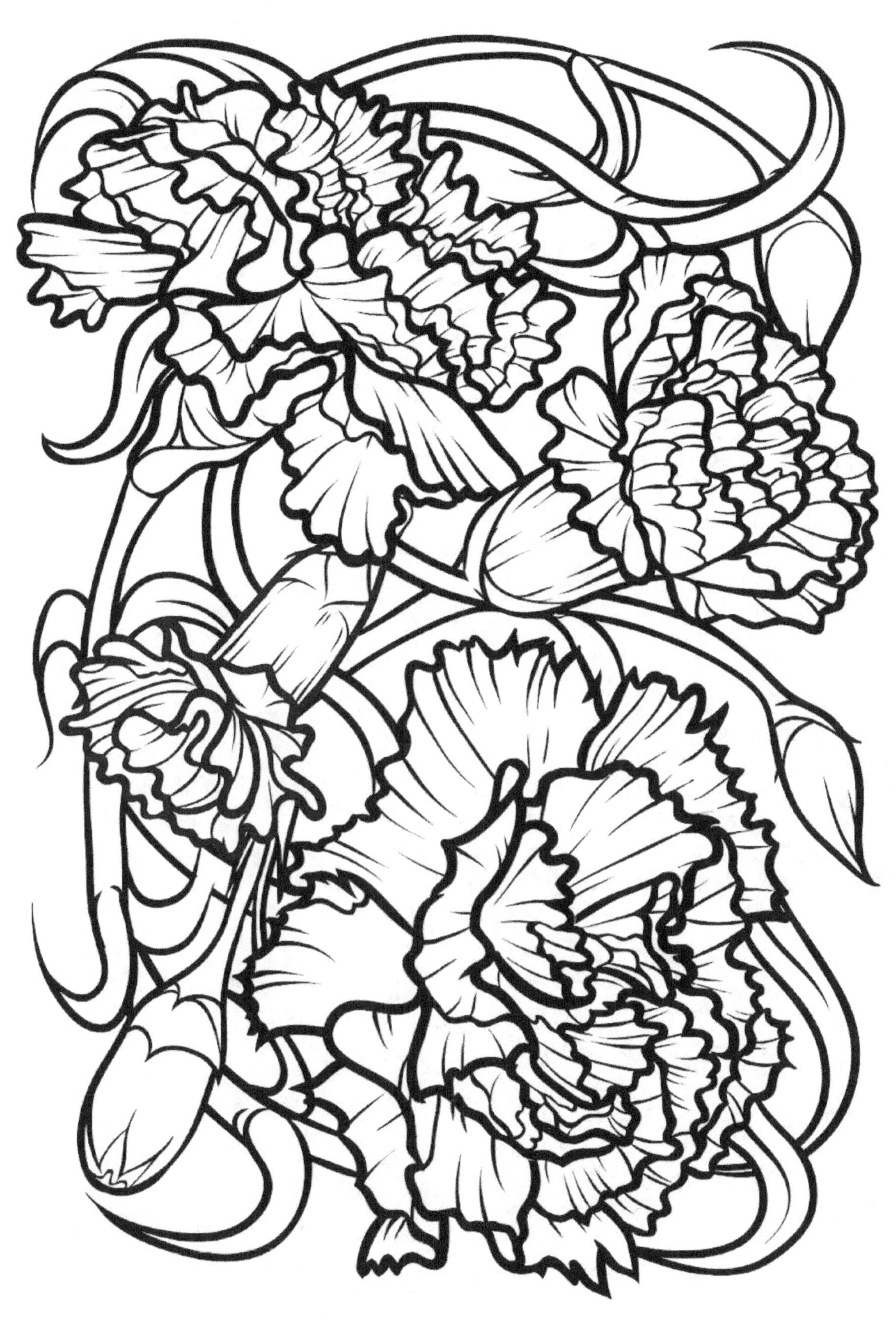

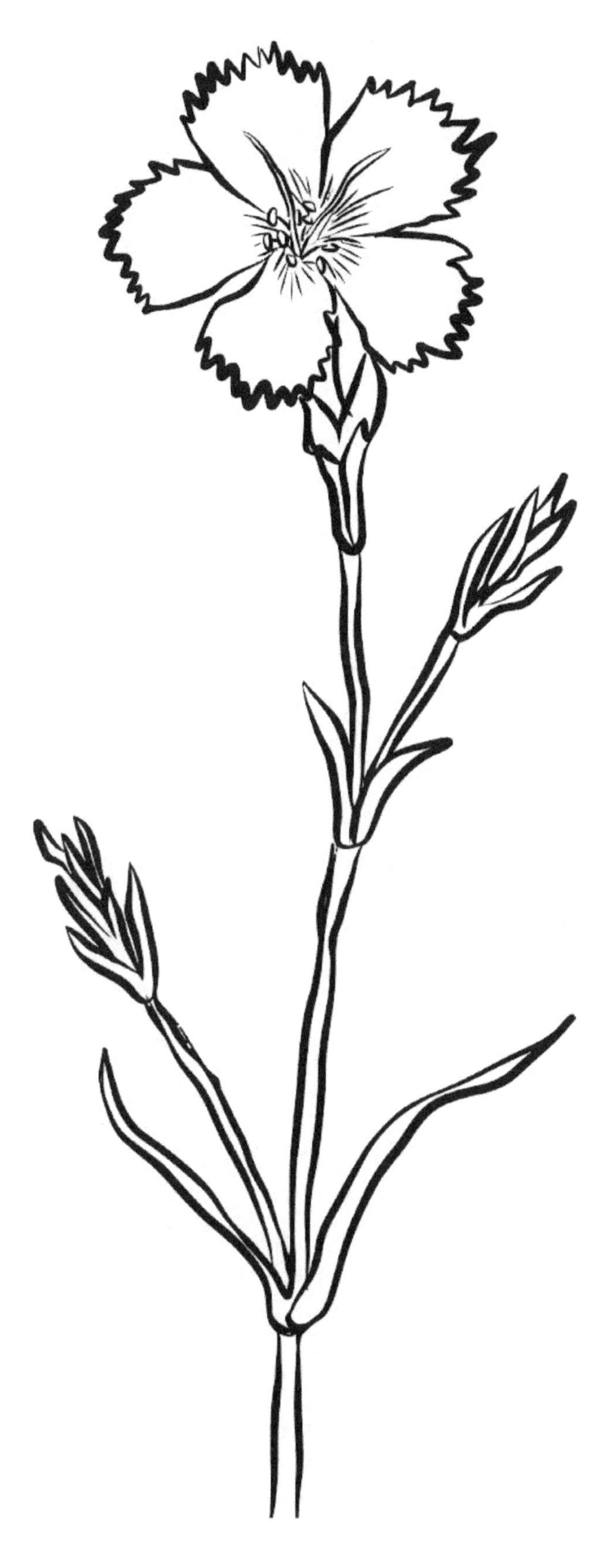

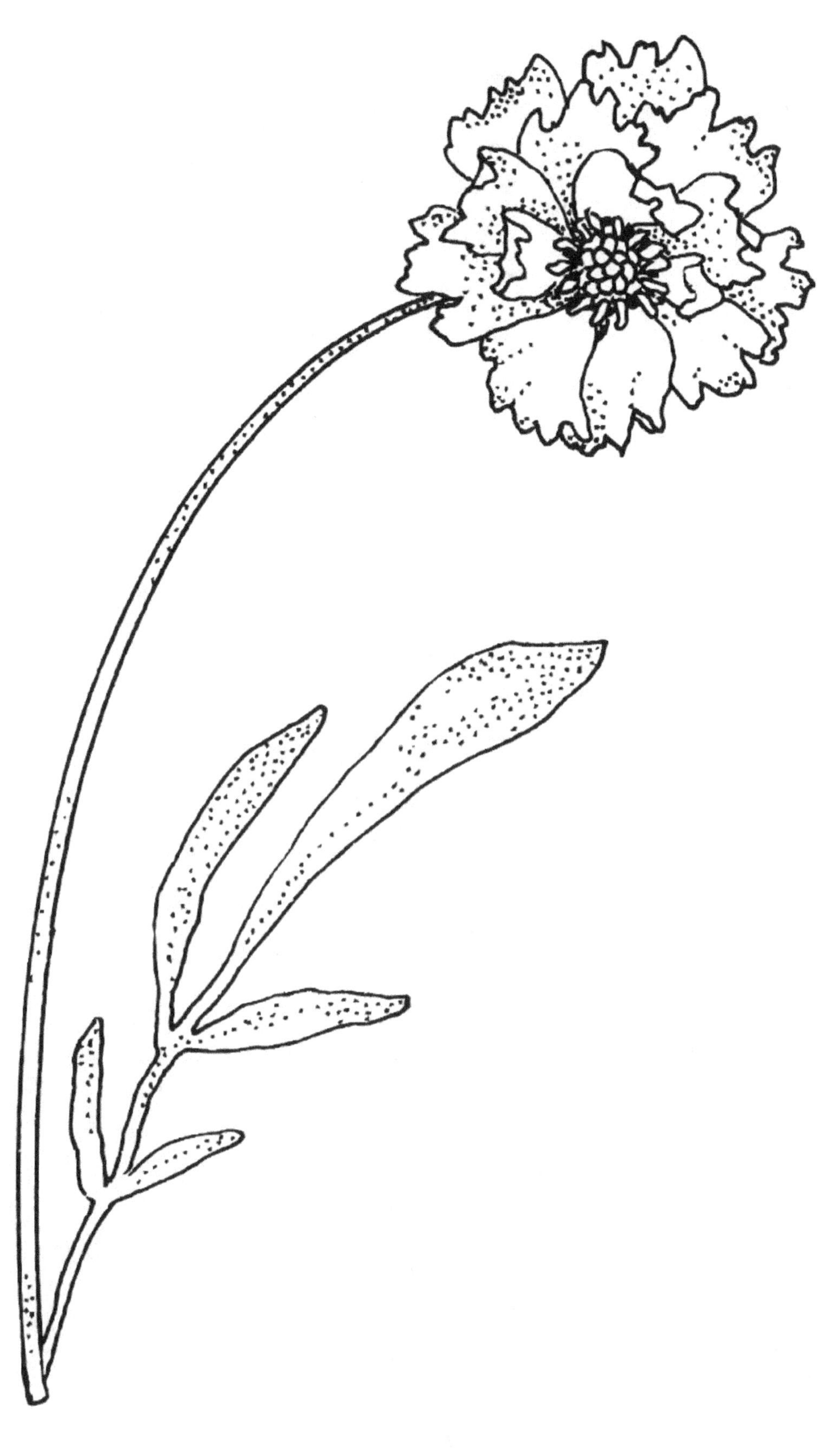

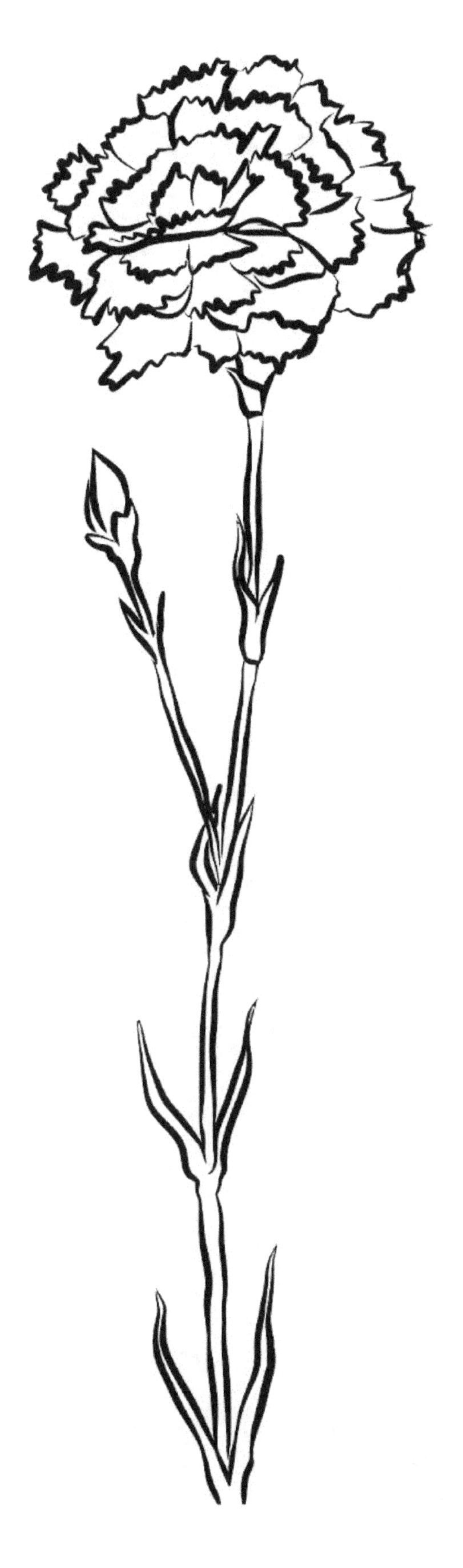

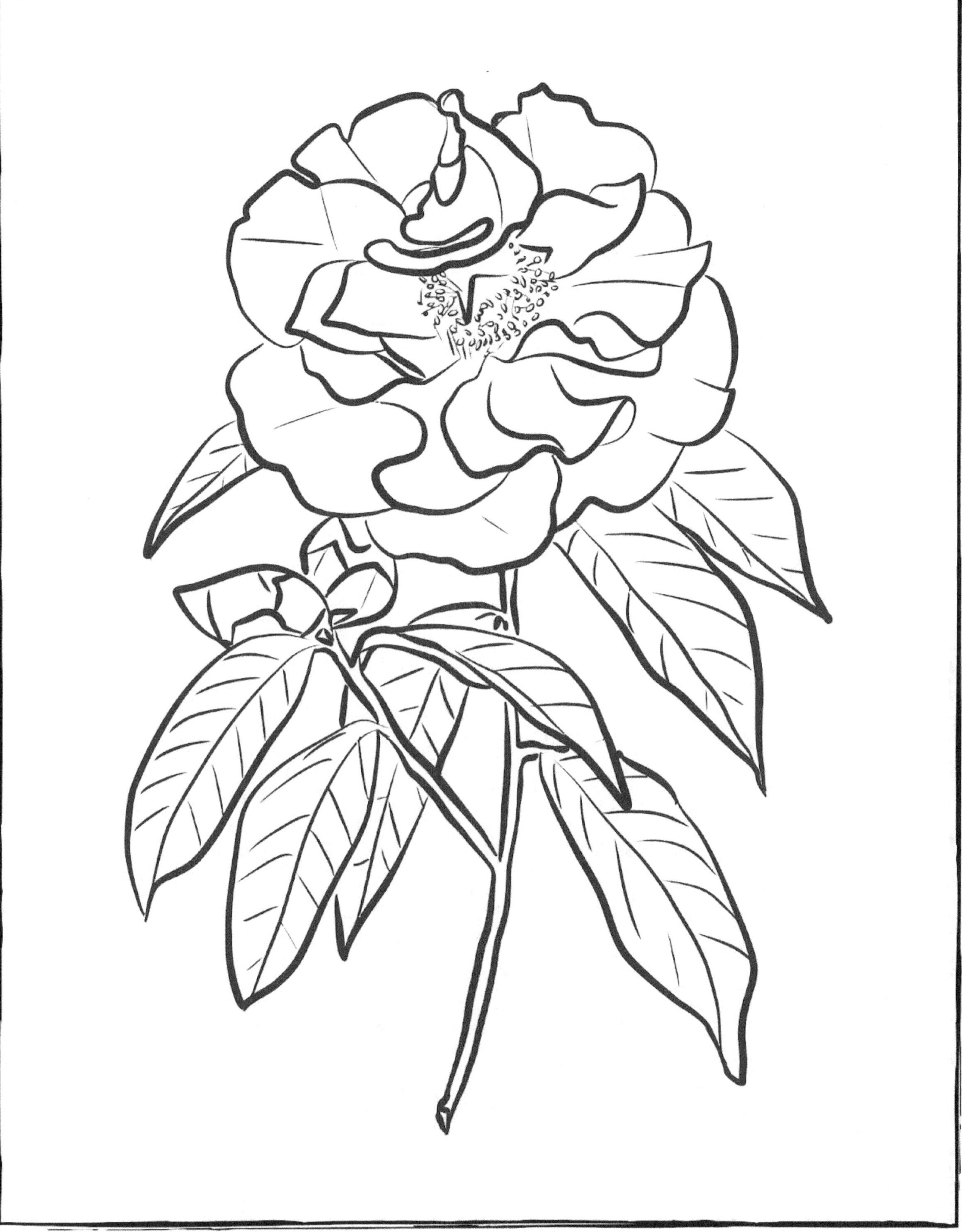

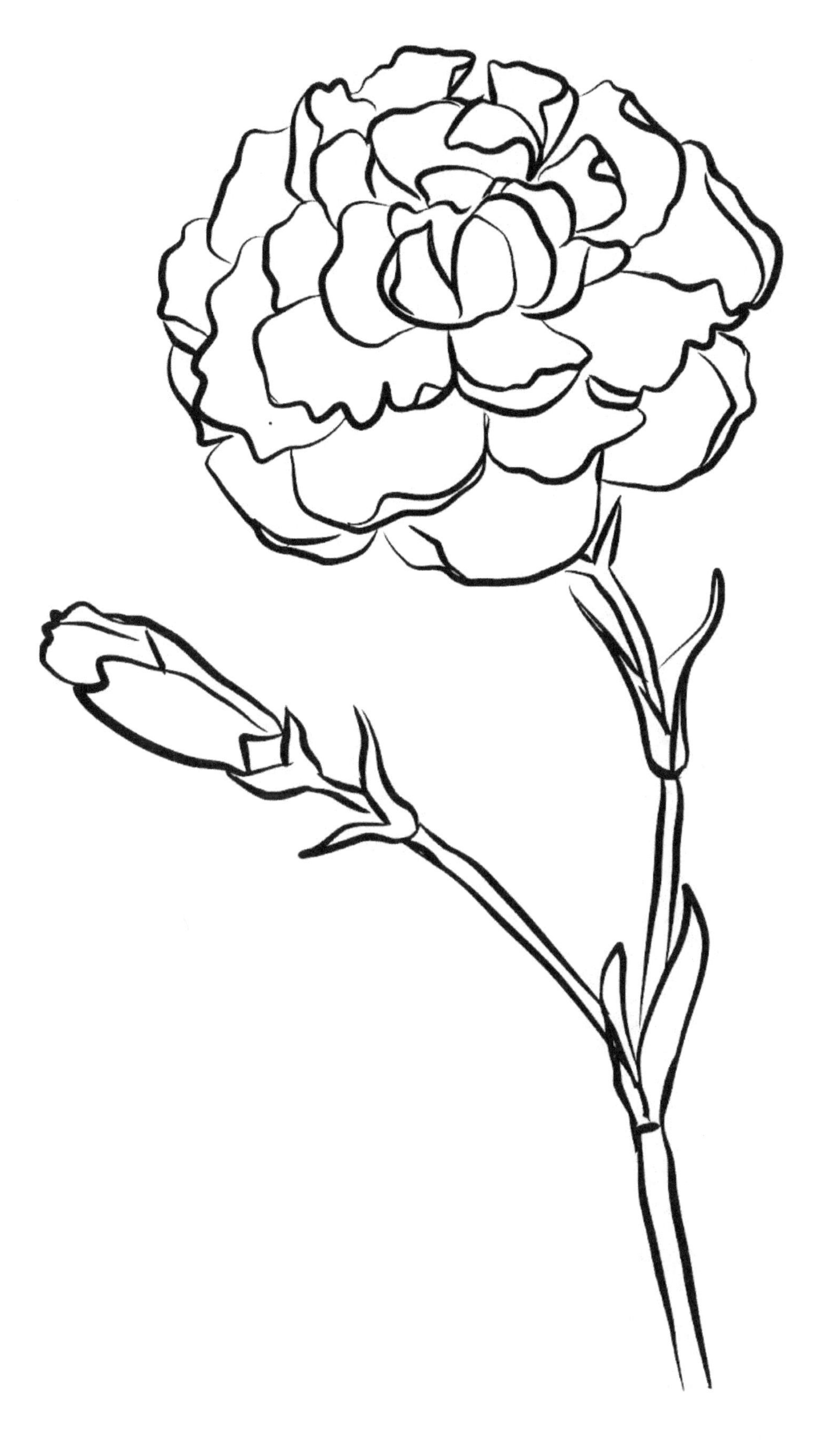

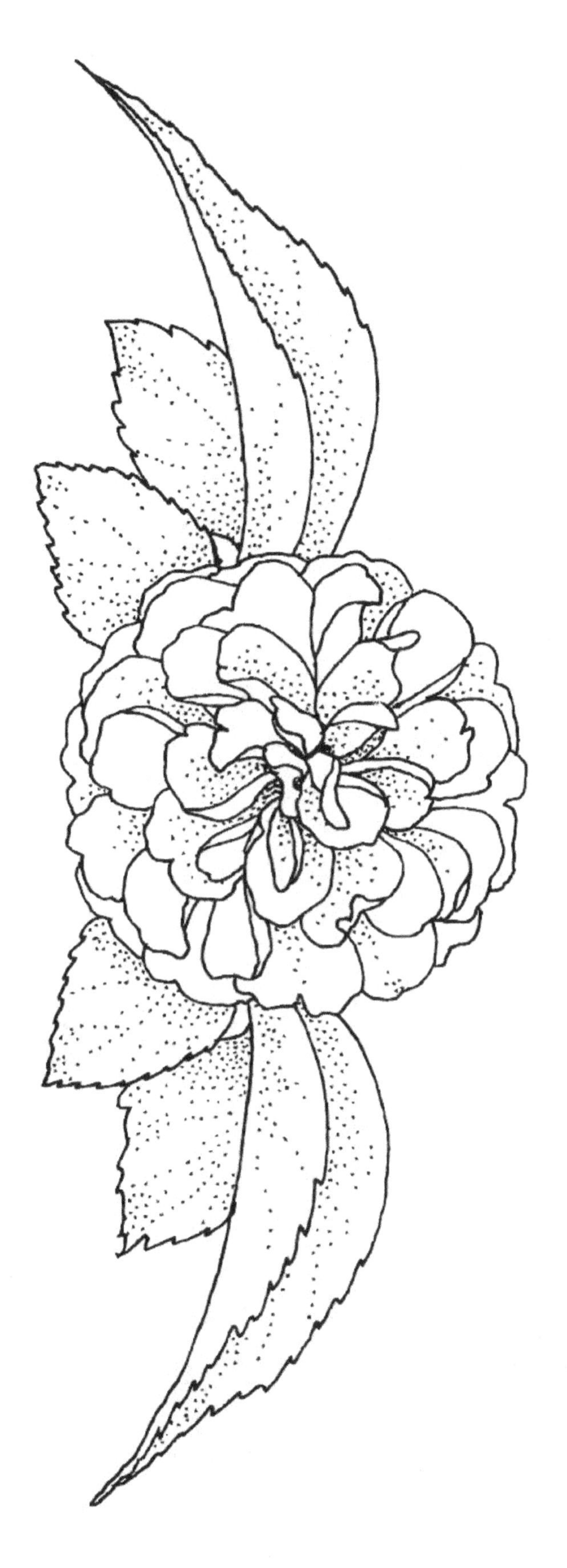

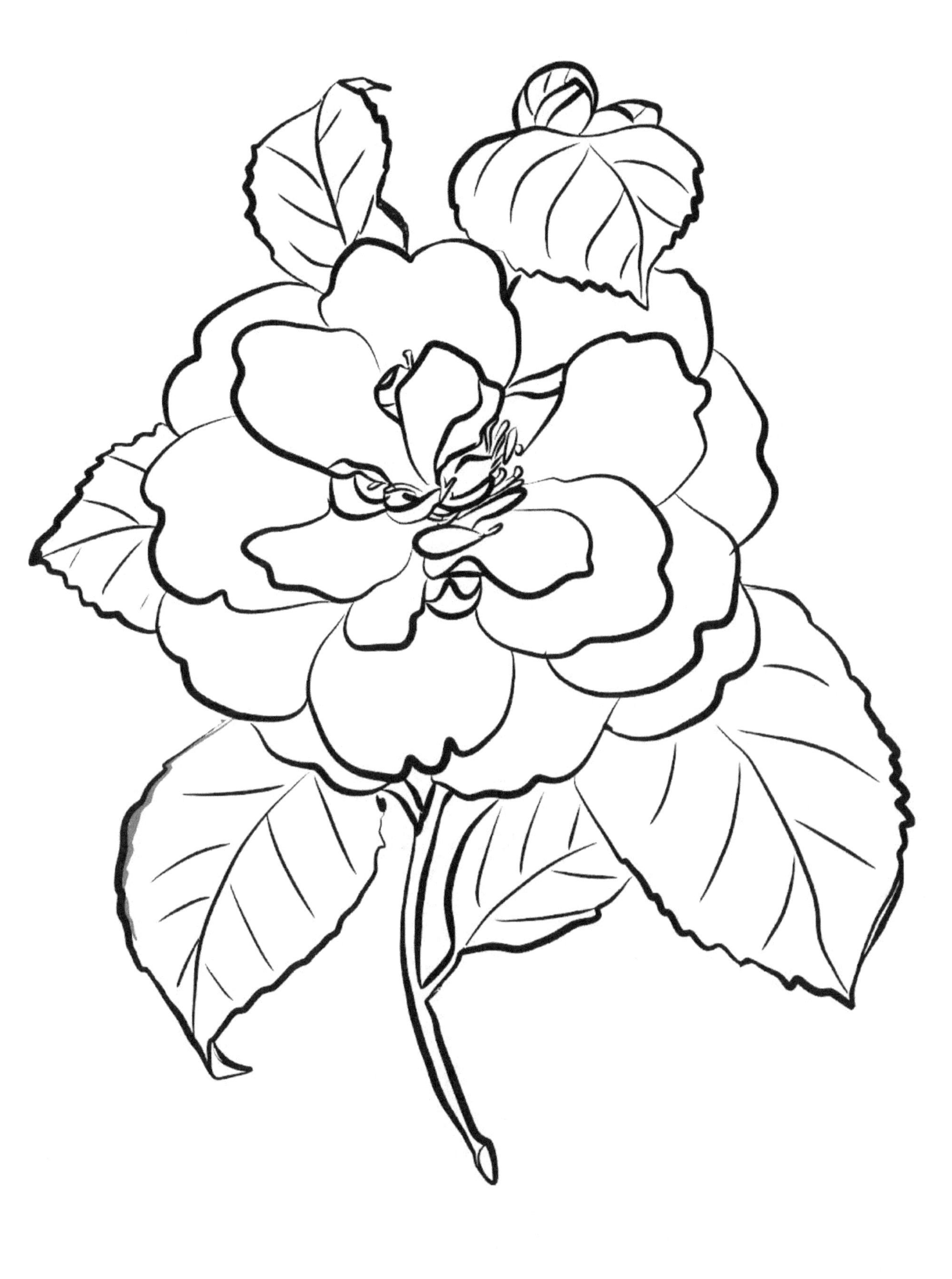

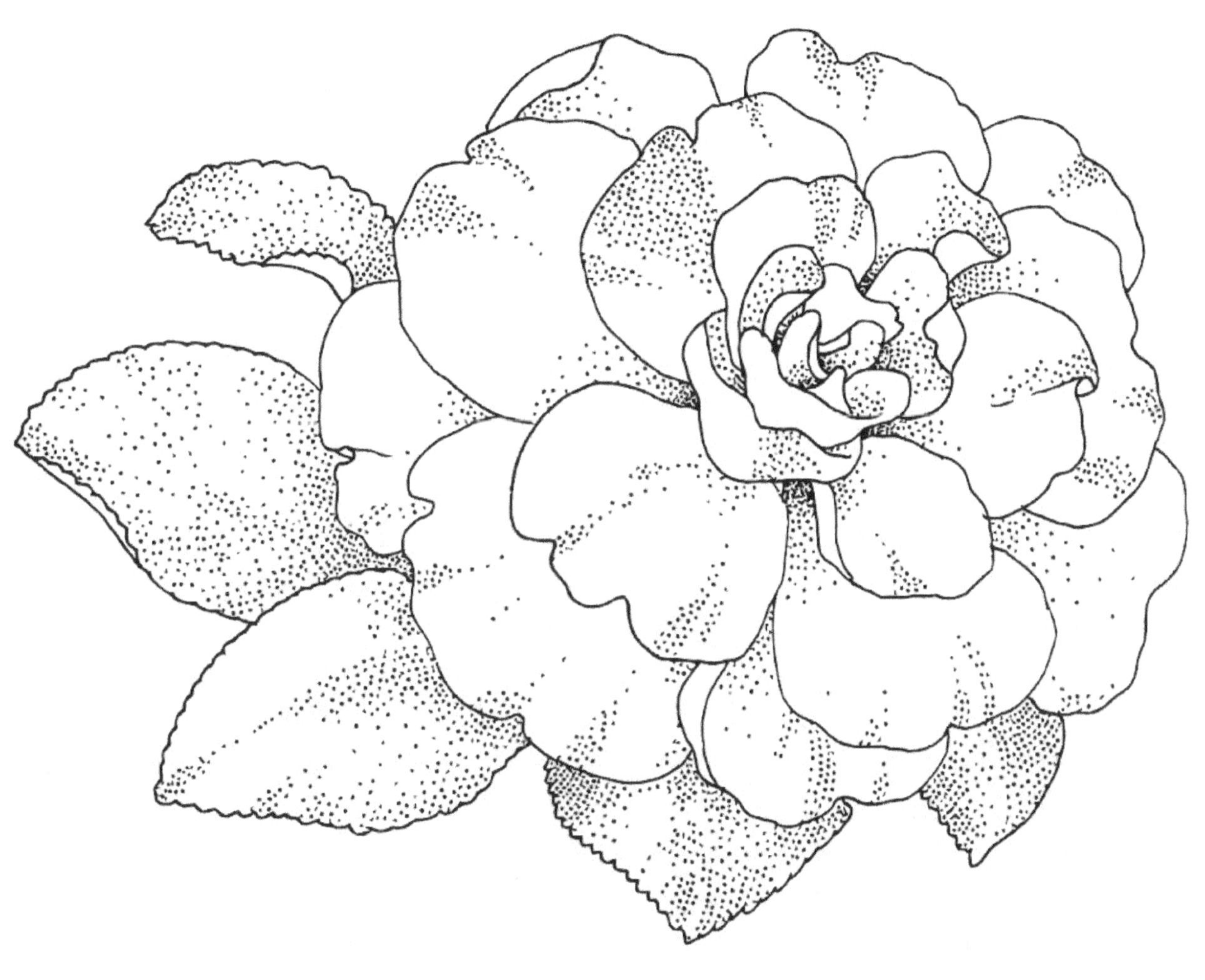

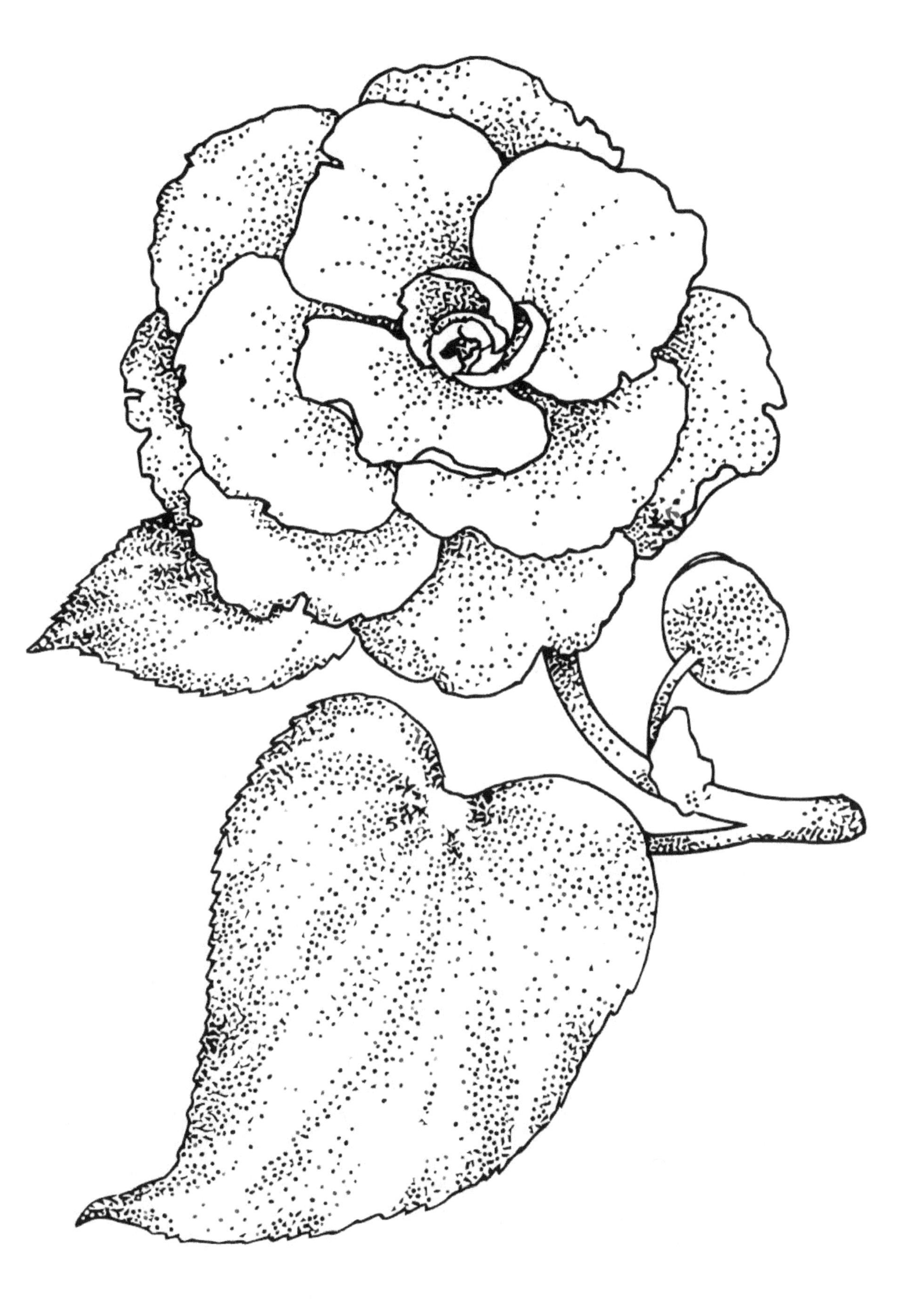

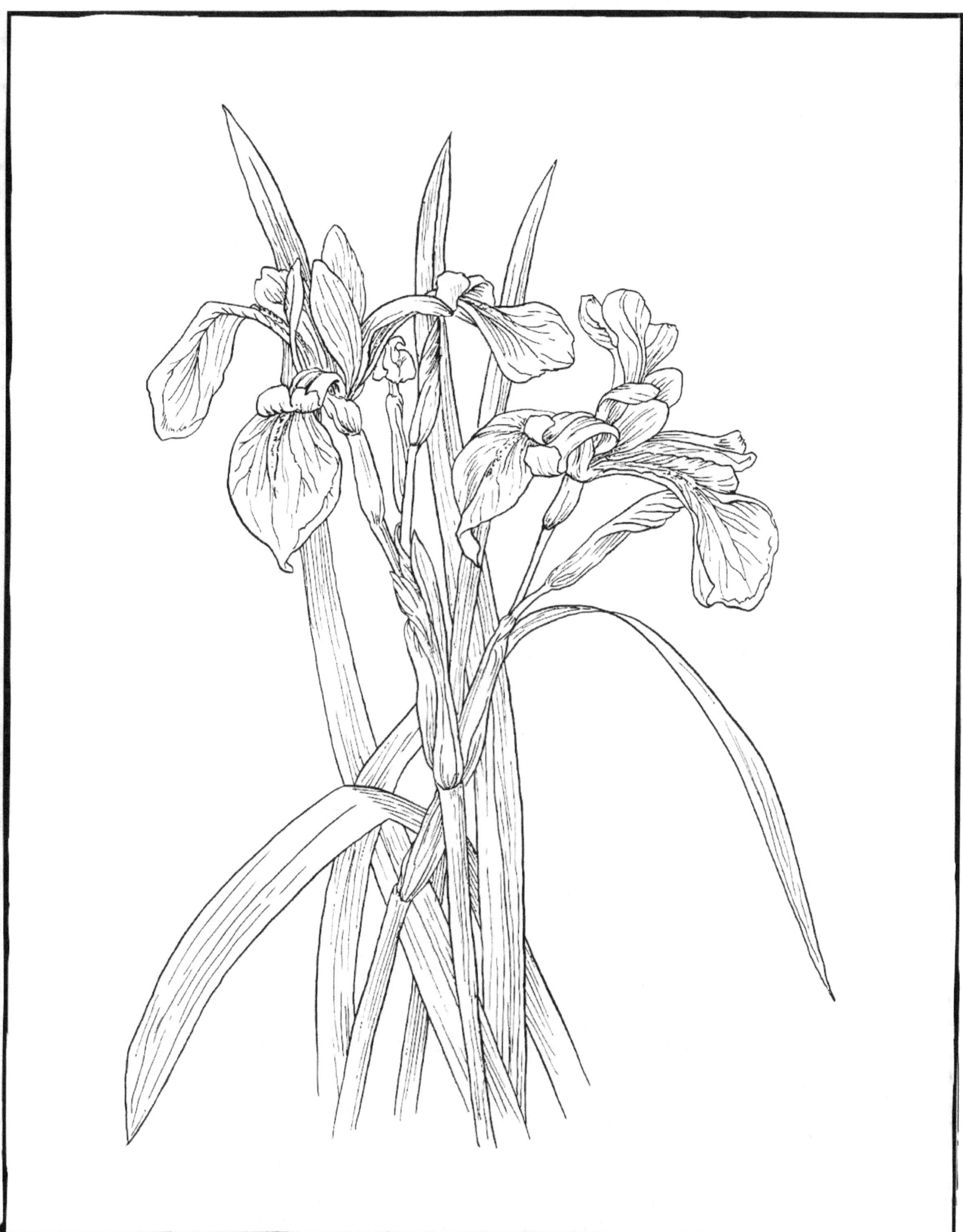

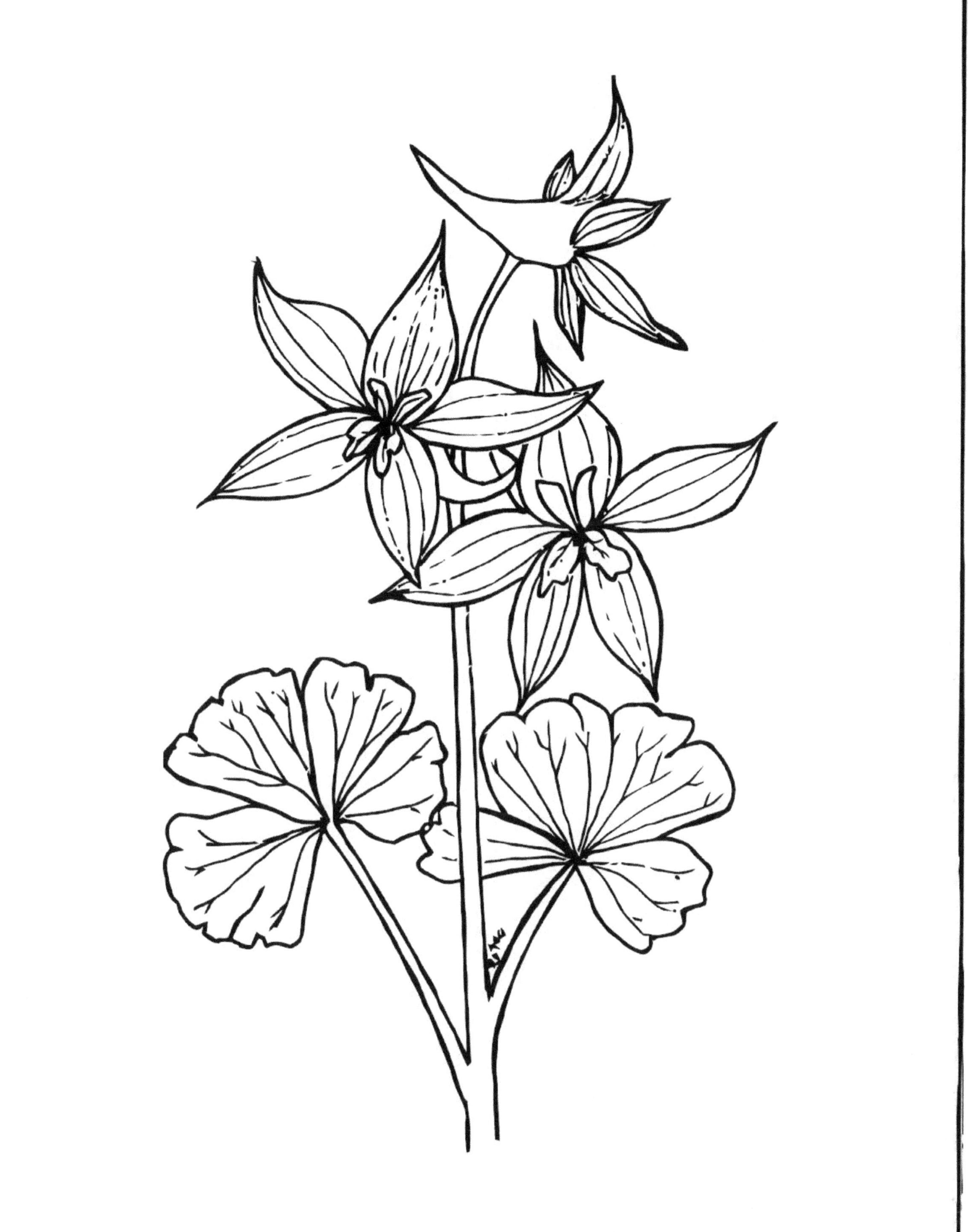